STRESS-FREE HOMESCHOOLING
Getting It All Done & Enjoying It!

Robin Gilman

Stress-Free Homeschooling: Getting It All Done & Enjoying It!
Copyright © 2017 Robin Gilman
All rights reserved.

No part of this book may be reproduced in any manner whatsoever without written permission of the publisher except in brief quotations embodied in critical articles or reviews. For information, write Robin Gilman, P.O. Box 447, Ottawa, Ontario, Canada K2S 1A6.

Web site: www.stressfreehomeschooling.com

Scripture quotations unless otherwise indicated are from The Holy Bible, English Standard Version® (ESV®), copyright © 2001 by Crossway, a publishing ministry of Good News Publishers. Used by permission. All rights reserved.

Scripture quotation marked "CEB" is taken from the Common English Bible, copyright © 2011 by Common English Bible. Used by permission. All rights reserved.

Scripture quotation marked "NIV" is taken from the Holy Bible, New International Version®, NIV® Copyright ©1973, 1978, 1984, 2011 by Biblica, Inc.® Used by permission. All rights reserved worldwide.

Printed by CreateSpace, An Amazon.com Company

ISBN-10: 1544958838

ISBN-13: 978-1544958835

DEDICATION

To my husband, Alan, who first introduced the concept of homeschooling to me, and who has walked this journey with me as an incredibly involved husband and father to our children.

And to our ten children, thought of and created by God, each one special and each enriching our family in their own unique way.

CONTENTS

ACKNOWLEDGMENTS	7
WHY YOU SHOULD READ THIS BOOK	9
INTRODUCTION	11
CHAPTER 1: YOU CAN DO IT	13
CHAPTER 2: ANSWERS TO COMMON STRESSES	29
CHAPTER 3: PRIORITIES	39
CHAPTER 4: REALISTIC EXPECTATIONS	53
CHAPTER 5: GETTING IT ALL DONE (NON-ACADEMIC)	63
CHAPTER 6: GETTING IT ALL DONE (ACADEMICS)	83
CHAPTER 7: LIFE LEARNING	101
CHAPTER 8: FINANCES	125
CHAPTER 9: SCHEDULES	133
CHAPTER 10: ENJOYING IT!	141
APPENDIX A: SCRIPTURE TO MEMORIZE WITH YOUR CHILDREN	155
APPENDIX B: INEXPENSIVE RECIPES	157
APPENDIX C: RECOMMENDED BOOKS TO READ ALOUD	163
ABOUT THE AUTHOR	169

ACKNOWLEDGMENTS

First, I am so grateful for my husband, Alan, for his involvement in the writing, formatting, and publishing of this book. He has been instrumental in making this happen.

I cannot adequately thank Cathie Currey, my friend since our teenage years, who rose up in the eleventh hour to edit this book. She was also the prime instrument of the Lord in my coming to faith so many decades ago and we have walked together, encouraging each other in the journey of life (including homeschooling) since then.

And most of all, thanks be to God, my Rock and my Strength, my very trustworthy heavenly Father, who has lead us and guided us in this wonderful journey with His infinite patience, faithfulness and love.

WHY YOU SHOULD READ THIS BOOK

By Alan Gilman

If you are a homeschooler or prospective homeschooler, this may be one of the most important books you will ever read! Within these pages, my wife, Robin, shares some of the practical wisdom she has gained from over thirty years of home-educating our ten children.

Many parents homeschool because we believe that our children's education is primarily our responsibility. Who else can better teach them to discover their God-given gifts and talents, training them "in the way they should go" (Proverbs 22:6; CEB)? Yet we still allow the expectations of society, family, and friends, instead of God, to set insurmountable goals that cannot be achieved. It isn't too long before discouragement sets in and we are tempted to give up.

Robin has been graced with the ability to focus on what's really important in life, keeping the main thing the main thing. Like Jesus's words to Martha, who was "anxious and troubled about many things" (Luke

10:41), Robin will remind you of what is truly necessary to effectively homeschool your children. From academic goals, household management, and your marriage, to your own spiritual and physical well-being, you will learn helpful—even life-saving—practical tips that will help you endure and keep your sanity along the way.

Throughout this book, you will meet some of my most favorite people, our kids, many of whom are currently doing some extraordinary things. We hope and pray that you will be encouraged by ordinary parents such as we, who, in spite of making more than our share of mistakes, are so grateful for how God's blessing has been upon each one of our children as he has prepared them to do his will in the world.

Don't think that "Stress-Free Homeschooling" means that homeschooling is easy. Raising children is hard work, but it shouldn't be made more difficult by turning it into something it doesn't need to be. Robin will help you discover how to best homeschool your children without the extra burden of unnecessary stress.

INTRODUCTION

It was almost time for me to begin my seminar at the annual homeschool conference, and people were still thronging into the room. I kept my eye on the door and on the clock. It was time to begin, and the instructions left on the podium for the speaker said to begin on time, but people were still entering en masse. I waited a couple of minutes, and then the gentleman who was recording the seminar said I should begin. So I did.

I was told later that they had to turn people away. It wasn't because I am a famous speaker; I am not. But what this showed me is that the topic of my seminar, *Stress-Free Homeschooling – Getting it all Done and Enjoying it!*, is one that homeschool parents feel that they need.

Throughout the following day many people told me how my talk encouraged them. And one woman asked me to write a book.

That is where this book comes from.

Homeschooling *is* a large task. There are many reasons that parents stress over this task. I have written this book to help you realize that you can homeschool

Introduction

without undue stress. You can get it all done, and yes, you can even enjoy it!

CHAPTER 1: YOU CAN DO IT

I was innocent. I was naïve. I thought what I was about to do was no big deal. After all, I had read a book which gave me the impression that the path that we were embarking on was natural and normal. Besides, I had two friends who were doing it: homeschooling.

This was back in the mid-'80s, when most people hadn't heard of homeschooling. That was confirmed by the wide-eyed, shocked reactions I received when I mentioned that we were homeschooling our five year old.

"Do you have a teaching degree?" was the first question that came out of the mouths of flabbergasted friends, acquaintances, and strangers when they found out I was actually committing such folly.

"No, one doesn't need a teaching degree," I smiled. "I can read and I love my child." I got this reply (along with my confidence) straight from that one book I had read: *Home Spun Schools*.

This is certainly true. In some ways, not having a teaching degree can be an asset in the context of homeschooling. One of the things one learns with such a degree is how to teach in a classroom within the institutional structure. Many moms with teaching degrees who have worked in schools and then begun teaching their own children at home have found themselves imitating the classroom setting, which isn't necessary, and can sometimes be detrimental.

Instead of teaching a class of twenty-five students at different readiness levels, a mom (or dad or both) is teaching her child(ren) one-on-one and able to teach to the level of that particular child.

A couple of decades later, that same daughter with whom we began our homeschooling journey, Sarah, went to Haiti as a missionary, in response to an email invitation to teach at a small school run by Youth With A Mission (YWAM). The email said that having been homeschooled would be an asset, since homeschoolers tend to be self-starters.

Sarah ended up teaching at that school in Haiti for her first nine months there. She didn't find her lack of a teaching degree to be a hindrance, as a Canadian teaching degree wouldn't have been a help in this different culture. Sarah was able to get to know her students and work with the materials they had in the unique setting that she was in.

The homeschool parent has the advantage of knowing her students very well and using materials that are best suited for them in their unique home setting.

If you can read, you can learn along with your child. I have learned so much more since I have been homeschooling my children than when I was in school. For one thing, being more mature, with more life experience, I am far more interested in learning and I have far more reference points or "hooks" on which to hang new information.

Loving your child(ren) and being able to read are the two essential ingredients for homeschooling your child(ren). A teaching degree…not so much.

"What about socialization?" was the usual next question. My daughter was very shy. "School would bring her out of herself," I was told by well-meaning people.

Really? I had been shy as a child and teenager. School didn't change me. Very gradually, as I grew, and more especially with my first part-time job and through other life experiences, I overcame my shyness to the point that my children can't believe I ever *was* shy.

Fast forwarding to the present, that is exactly what happened with some of my children who were painfully shy. They gradually overcame it through life ex-

Chapter 1: You Can Do It

periences as they grew. They didn't need school or *negative* socialization for that. In fact they were blessed not to have had such experiences as I did, when a girl in seventh grade got the whole class making fun of me for my mispronunciation of the "s" sound.

Traumatic incidents aside, I did well in school and was a teacher-pleasing "A" student, who found out what the teachers wanted and gave it to them without necessarily learning a whole lot. While I am grateful that I learned to read, write, and do basic arithmetic, there was an awful lot of wasted time, and regurgitation of facts that I didn't use and didn't remember after the tests (which I did well on).

But I had never heard of another option until my husband came home and told me he had heard a certain Dr. Raymond Moore on a Focus on the Family broadcast, who had been talking about educating one's children by "homeschooling." My initial reaction wasn't positive. I had never heard of this way of educating one's children. But with some discussion and prayer, it seemed like a desirable option. Then I found out that two of my friends were homeschooling; one lent me Dr. Moore's book, and after reading it I was more convinced than ever that this was not only possible, but positively the best option, given our goals for our children.

With the teaching degree question out of the way, and the socialization objection temporarily taken care of (that objection was to resurface continually for the next few decades), I informed my parents of our plans.

The first words out of my father's mouth were, "Don't you have to be (ahem) *organized*, to do that?" Ouch.

I'm not the most disorganized person, but I guess organization wasn't my strong point.

Re-read that last sentence, and take comfort. Say to yourself, "If that woman, without a teaching diploma and weak in the area of organization can homeschool, so can I."

I have had so many people exclaim, when they hear that I have ten children and have homeschooled them all, "You must be so organized!"

"Not really", I confess. "But I have grown in that area." And I have. I have grown in many areas, but I am still not super-organized. I like to plan, but I don't always stick to the plan.

When we began homeschooling in the '80s, we purchased a phonics program and a math curriculum. Guided by these resources, I wasn't having to organize, or invent how and what to teach, but simply followed the directions. I could do that, you see, because I could read. ☺

Chapter 1: You Can Do It

I didn't have to spend a lot of time in formal academics when teaching our five year old, and had plenty of time to spend doing all the other things that a pregnant mother of two small girls does. Our second daughter was three years old at that time.

It was when our third child was born that life became really busy. That was the most difficult season in my mothering: having three children ages five and under. It got easier after that, even with more children. But I call those earlier years the foggy years, where I was constantly sleep deprived—most of my children didn't sleep through the night until I decided that they were going to do so at age one. As children grow older, they become more helpful, not to mention more reasonable, and so by the time our fourth was born and our eldest was seven, things were more manageable. And as I mentioned, it only got better/easier as they grew up and God blessed us with more children.

I should clarify that while children become more helpful because they are more able, we need to do our part in teaching them to be helpful. This is an essential component of their education; or in other words, part of our discipling them. They are learning valuable concepts such as "everyone helps."

For the next couple of decades, I was most often either pregnant or had a nursing baby, along with a toddler, a preschooler, and one learning to read (code for "needs Mom for all schooling as opposed to working independently"), as well as some older ones, who could do some independent work. I often felt as though I were juggling balls, and sometimes dropping them. But I didn't really sweat it—I just picked up those balls and kept on juggling.

I admit that the reason I didn't "sweat it" or stress when I "dropped some balls," that is, when I didn't get everything done that I would have liked to, is partly due to my laid-back nature—however, I believe that even if that isn't your nature, there are things that will help you overcome a natural tendency to stress. I will address this in the following chapters.

I tell people that I feel with all that busyness I gave my children a bare-bones academic education. That is, I taught them the essentials: to love God and His Word, to do "reading, 'riting, and 'rithmetic, and to think. Yes, some years we did other subjects such as science, history, geography, or French. And I read to them *a lot*, because I love to read aloud to my children. I found out later how extremely beneficial it is to read to your children, but I was simply doing it because I enjoyed it that much!

While I consider that I gave my children this bare-bones academic education, I have wondered how those among my children who went on to college and university did so well and received scholarships (I say bare-bones *academic* education, because as I will explain in Chapter 7, "Life Learning," our children learn so very much from daily living and interacting with their parents and others). After giving it some thought, I believe I know the answer: we *taught our children to read and to think*. If they can read and think, then they can learn anything without much help.

A university professor was answering some questions for a research project that one of my sons did in college. Joshua was researching how institutions of higher learning were admitting homeschoolers. He asked this particular university professor (a homeschool dad himself) what were the pros and cons of homeschool vs. the pros and cons of public school. The professor waxed eloquent on the negatives of public school, and then my son asked, "But what are the positives of public school?" The professor thought, and thought, and thought, and then said, "Well, if the parents both *have* to work—No!" he interrupted himself. "The child is better off sitting in the living room reading a book than going to public school."

This professor had spent years watching students enter university after high school, and his observation was that while the students could decode the words, that is they could read them, they couldn't interact with them. They couldn't think. (Note: obviously, this doesn't refer to *all* students, but according to this professor, the majority.)

So even though I didn't give our children the amazing educational experience that I know some homeschooling parents give their children—building their own telescopes, making a model of the ancient pyramids, visiting amazing historical sites—even though I was juggling babies and toddlers and all manner of children, plus various life interruptions (did I mention that we moved across this vast country of Canada four times?), our children grew up to be successful adults.

By a "successful adult" I mean one who can function well in society, communicate effectively, is considerate of other people, does meaningful work whether through a career, a ministry, parenting, volunteering, etc., and who loves God and wants to follow and serve Him.

My own experience, as well as that of countless others, demonstrates that an ordinary person can home educate their children, even though we all have weaknesses.

I have already alluded (thanks, Dad!) to the fact that I am not by nature organized. I may not be on the opposite end of the spectrum, but organization is certainly not among my strengths. While I enjoy clean, tidy, and neat, that's not my priority. I would rather read books to my children than have a spotless house.

I tend to have piles here and there (counter top, desk, etc.). I am flexible, which can be good, or not. For example, each year, no, each semester(!) I have worked diligently to make a great daily school schedule. This schedule worked beautifully...for two days. I eventually managed to keep rigidly to my schedule for three weeks, and then rather loosely after that.

I made chore charts that we stuck to quite nicely, but I found that with the abundance of life in our home, the daily school schedules I made were too tight, with too little margin. For example, perhaps most days, a certain child could complete their arithmetic in the time allotted for that subject, but then would come a day when that child had difficulty, needing more time than usual for me to help him over that hump, and that would take us off-schedule.

Or one of my children would be having what are called "character issues," such as a bad attitude, or two of my children would be having problems with each other, and we would have to stop our academic pursuits so that I could walk them through those issues.

If we understand that one of the advantages of homeschooling is being able to stop and take time to further explain or help someone as needed, we need not stress about it. Instead, we can realize that these are wonderful educational moments and be thankful for them. And we can just pick up with the rest of the day, perhaps deferring something that we had planned for that day to the following day.

Before I had children, I thought I was a very patient person. And then I had children, including colicky babies who cried when I wanted to sleep. Oh, the impatience that rose up within me! But God uses our children (among other things) to reveal our sin nature to us. That's a good thing! When that sin rises up and stares us in the face, we can deal with it, that is repent and ask God for His help in that particular area. Yes, children are great for our sanctification!

Having children and homeschooling them has helped me to grow in patience, in maintaining the house (I have a lot more growth to do in that area), and even in organization.

You might find that (as is the case with my husband, Alan, and me) some of your weak areas are your spouse's strengths, and vice versa. This can be of great benefit to your children. In our case, it took us a while to really appreciate these different traits in each other, as we tend to think the way we are is the right or better way. But at this point, we can appreciate and benefit from each other's strengths and differences.

In our home, while the three R's and other academic subjects have, for the most part, been taught by me, Alan has played a critical role in our children's discipleship/education. Remember how I concluded that our children were successful in their post-secondary education because we taught them to read and think? My husband has played a huge role in teaching our children to think, as he has had countless conversations with our various children, whether one-on-one, or with a few of them at a time, or around the dinner table.

But it is not just we parents who have initiated all the learning that has taken place in our home. Our children themselves have had various interests that they have brought to our family. For example, many years ago Alan and I did not concern ourselves with politics, until Daniel, at around age thirteen, became interested in a certain Christian politician and began telling us about him, asking us to watch some of his speeches on the Internet.

That is when our family's interest in politics began. We lived in Vancouver at that time, but we eventually ended up in Ottawa, the capital of Canada, and when Daniel was in university, he worked for various federal politicians part time. Our whole family knows far more about politics than we would have if Daniel hadn't sparked that interest in us.

Homeschooled children have more free time than their peers, as their academic subjects can be completed in less time than if they attended a school. This leaves them free to pursue, and excel in, their various interests.

Many of our children have pursued ballet in a Christian context. Not only have they had the time, thanks to being homeschooled, to pursue excellence in this art form, but most of them have been able to teach as well, first in a small studio in our home, and then as this studio was taken out of our home and expanded under the vision of our second daughter. (This Christian dance school is called "Arise School of Dance").

Have you ever noticed that what parents do, children will often imitate, and even expand upon? And it seems logical that the more our children are around us, the more they will be influenced, even unintentionally, by us.

One example of this concerns our pro-life stance. Over the years, I took our children to annual pro-life marches and to "life chains" (where one stands on street corners with pro-life signs, praying silently).

Two of our children became heavily involved in the pro-life cause. Unbeknownst to me, Daniel and Devorah used to get together as children and pray for the end of abortion. Daniel worked extensively with the pro-life group on his university campus and has been a sought after speaker in the pro-life movement. Devorah now works full time for the Canadian Centre for

Bioethical Reform, a pro-life group dedicated to ending abortion, where she speaks to audiences across Canada and leads life-saving activism projects.

So while we as homeschoolers want to be diligent to teach our children whatever academics they need to know, much learning takes place outside of that official context. Whether it be in informal conversations, or by our children pursuing what interests them, they will learn so much that isn't initiated by us.

I believe a lot of this is initiated by God, who gifts our children in various ways, and who has different callings for them to pursue.

In various areas that our children have pursued, they know so much more than we, their homeschooling parents.

God has brought various adults along at different times to invest in their lives, whether it was the woman who had a passion for birds at a time when our son, Jonathan, had a keen interest in them, or someone to mentor our daughter Tikvah in music just when she was developing a desire to learn more in that area, or a dad who taught Joshua some handyman skills in exchange for his daughter's dance classes.

God loves our children even more than we do. He cares for them, and as we seek Him, He will give us what we need in order to teach and disciple them. He will see that they have all that they need to fulfill His plans for them.

I am excited to share in the following pages some of what I have learned in the thirty-one years that I have been homeschooling, but above all I want you to know that if I, an ordinary Mom with strengths and weaknesses like anyone else, can by the grace of God homeschool my children, so can you!

CHAPTER 2: ANSWERS TO COMMON STRESSES

"I *do* want to homeschool David," my friend told me earnestly. "But I am terrified of math!" Eva perched on the kitchen stool, looking at me with her feelings of inadequacy written all over her face. She had taught high school English until her first child was born, and yet feared to homeschool her little boy, because of her perceived inability to handle math. "Eva," I assured her, "David is three and a half years old. You know enough to teach him his numbers. You can teach him 2 + 2, and you can even use curriculum that will help you in this. You will learn with him, and when it gets too hard for you, Eric (her husband) can help, or there are various curricula that have DVDs David can watch to learn, and people he can contact for help. There is also online learning for when he gets older."

Many conversations with many homeschoolers and wanna-be homeschoolers in many different cities throughout the decades have shown me that we all have similar concerns. Such as:

CAN I ACTUALLY TEACH MY CHILDREN?

If you are a parent, you already teach your children. You teach them to pick up their toys, to go to the toilet, to say "please" and "thank you," to look both ways when they cross the street, and so much more. Teaching your children is a natural part of what being a parent is. It doesn't stop when they reach four or five years old. Young children need only twenty or so minutes of formal academics a day, and you are more than adequate for this task. There is a plethora of curricula to choose from, although at a young age, a formal curriculum isn't even necessary as I will share in Chapter Six ("Getting it All Done—Academics").

Many people (such as my friend, Eva), have a certain subject (or several) that they are weak in and that they fear teaching. But all of us can teach our children the basics of reading, writing, and arithmetic, plus we can learn along with our children in other areas. Science is one of my weaker subjects, but when my five-year-old asked, "Mommy, where does the food go after it is in my mouth?" I said, "Let's look it up!" and we learned about the digestive system together. When our children are older, they can learn by themselves, getting help online or from others who are more expert in a field in which we are weak or ignorant.

Will our children get into university or college?

After many years of homeschooled students excelling in their university/college studies, many of these institutions are now welcoming them. In fact, the well-known speaker/science curriculum writer Dr. Jay Wile (http://www.drwile.com/about.html) first looked into homeschooling (eventually he and his wife homeschooled their daughter) because so many of his brightest science students in university had been homeschooled.

Will our children be successful (make it) in the real world?

Besides the example of my own children, I personally know many young adults who were homeschooled and are now doctors, accountants, teachers, business owners, pastors, missionaries, midwives, authors, carpenters, photographers, not to mention one of the noblest of all—homeschool moms!—these are not just making it in the real world; they are *world changers*!

What about socialization?

Many people are concerned about this issue, but as it turns out, children are best socialized by desirable adult role models, *not* their peers.

Note the following from an article by Dr. Raymond Moore:

Socialization. *We later became convinced that little children are not only better taught at home than at school, but also better socialized by parental example and sharing than by other little children. This idea was fed by many researchers from Tufts, Cornell, Stanford and California. Among the more prominent were (1) Urie Bronfenbrenner, who found that at least up to the sixth grade, children who spend less of their elective time with their parents than their peers tend to become peer-dependent; and (2) Albert Bandura who noted that this tendency has in recent years moved down to preschool,* **which in our opinion should be avoided whenever good parenting is possible**. *Contrary to common beliefs, little children are not best socialized by other kids; the more persons around them, the fewer meaningful contacts. We found that socialization is not neutral. It tends to be either positive or negative:* **Positive** *or altruistic and principled sociability is firmly linked with the family—with the quantity and quality of self-worth. This is in turn dependent largely on the track of values and experience provided by the family* **at least** *until the child can reason consistently. In other words, the child who works and eats and plays and has his rest and is read to daily, more with his parents than with his peers, senses that he is part of the family corporation—needed, wanted, depended upon. He is the one* *who has a sense of self-worth. (For full article, see: http://www.moorefoundation.com/article/50/faqs/synopsis)*

While non-homeschooled young people can have good social skills, when I meet a young person who doesn't look me in the eye when speaking with me, I tend to assume that they weren't homeschooled. Many people over the years have remarked to me and to other homeschooling moms I know how impressed they are with how our children and teens present themselves on the phone, at the reception desk at the dentist's office, and out and about interacting with people of all ages.

While this is obviously not true one hundred percent of the time, homeschooled young people tend to be comfortable interacting with *all* age groups—their own, younger children, older children, and adults—the real world isn't age segregated; this is something children learn in school.

How can I do it all? (Educating my children, shopping, laundry, cooking, cleaning)

While I do address this in detail in other chapters, I will summarize here by saying that your children's education will not be as time consuming as you might imagine. When they are young, twenty to thirty minutes of formal education a day is all they need. As they grow older, they can do much on their own. It takes less time for your child to learn a concept when they are being tutored one-on-one than in a classroom setting. Since they are not in a classroom with twenty or thirty other children, they don't need to waste their time on "busy" work (e.g. filling out workbook pages) which exists only because teachers are expected to handle more children than can effectively be managed at one time.

Concerning the rest of it—cleaning, laundry, shopping, etc.—this will necessitate family involvement/teamwork—which is a good thing for everyone!

WHAT IF MY PARENTS DON'T APPROVE

We all want our parents' approval, and some of them can voice their disapproval quite emphatically. In my generation homeschooling was in the pioneer stage, and there wasn't much documentation to prove its worth. My parents were quite concerned, as were some aunts and cousins who were teachers in the public education system.

I remember my father expressing his concern in the days before everyone had a computer (or several) in their home. He asked me how my children would learn about computers, which were just beginning to be used in schools. I assured him that my brother-in-law was a computer programmer and could teach my children what they would need to know, so they would be fine. Little did we know that before too long every home would have one or more computers and that it would be my children helping *me* with my computer and cell phone needs. In fact, I am amazed that even my younger children who don't go on the computer much at all seem to know intuitively how to help me navigate my technological devices.

My father worried about many aspects of his grandchildren's education. When my parents came over he would inevitably quiz my children on arithmetic, geography, and other subjects. While one of my daughters disliked this and told me that any time she happened to be left alone with her grandfather in a room, she left so as not to be quizzed, one of my sons thought it was fun—sort of a game.

While I felt somewhat upset over my parents' reaction, I eventually realized that it came out of love and concern—they wanted the best for their grandchildren, and didn't believe that they could get the best education at home.

However, since that time, a whole generation of homeschoolers has grown up and there are now statistics to show how well homeschoolers perform in university, college, and life! It is helpful to have some facts/statistics on hand to show the doubting parent.

Chapter 2: Answers to Common Stresses

The following is an eight-page article on "What Are They Doing Now" by Dr. Jay Wile that includes statistics on the success of homeschooled graduates. Some of your parents' concerns regarding higher education, whether or not their grandchildren will make it in the real world, and worries about socialization, are answered in this article:

http://www.drwile.com/what_now.pdf

Incidentally, because it has been proven over time, all of my previously doubting relatives who are teachers now think that homeschooling is a wonderful way to educate children.

If homeschooling continues to be a bone of contention between you and your parents, you can kindly tell them that you appreciate that they want the best for their grandchildren, but you are convinced that this is what *is* best for them, and ask them to respect your choice.

WHAT ABOUT MY MARRIAGE?

Your marriage is extremely important. I will discuss this in the following chapter on priorities.

WHAT ABOUT FINANCES?

If you are going to homeschool, then your family will probably not be functioning on two full-time salaries. While some moms homeschool while working part time, whether from home or not, a great number of homeschooling moms do not earn an income.

Many years ago, the husband of a homeschooling friend of mine thought that to make ends meet his wife needed to seek outside employment. My friend did some calculations and presented them to her husband. These calculations revealed the cost of her working: the clothing that she would need, the day-care costs for their younger children, as well as the costs associated with sending the other children to school, including the increased cost of purchasing more processed food, etc. As a result, her husband realized that the family would not be greatly benefitted financially, and agreed that his wife should stay at home and homeschool their children.

More on finances in chapter eight.

What about my sanity?

This is addressed in the next chapter as well as Chapters 4 and 10.

One last note: when I am writing about stress-free homeschooling, I am not saying that homeschooling is "tra-la-la-la, walking through fields of daisies and buttercups in the sunshine."

Parenting (which is discipling, which is what homeschooling is) can be challenging and extremely difficult at times. There will likely be days and seasons where you might feel "tra-la-la," but there will most assuredly be days and seasons where life is anything but that.

Even though this is the case, one can certainly homeschool (disciple) one's children without undue stress. More on this in chapter 10: "Enjoying It".

CHAPTER 3: PRIORITIES

"If you had asked me what my priority was, I would have said, 'God' ", the young man said. He was telling me about an impactful lecture he had heard about priorities. "But I see now, that in actuality, that hasn't been the case."

It is said that what you talk about often, what you spend your time, energy, and money on, reveal where your priorities lie.

I encourage you to pause and consider what your priorities are, from the angle that this young man shared with me: what do you spend your time, energy, money, and thoughts on? What do you *want* your priorities to be? It might possibly be time for some of us to refocus.

WHY DO YOU HOMESCHOOL?

A great piece of advice that was given to me as I began my homeschooling journey was to write down the reason I am homeschooling. This is something to discuss with your spouse, so that you are on the same page. It is important to know why you are homeschooling because that will inform what you do, what books or educational materials you use, and how much time you spend on different aspects of your children's education. And it gives you a ready answer for those who ask.

People have different reasons for educating their children at home. For some, it is because they believe that they can give their children a better education than the public schools can. Many parents have strong religious beliefs that the public school boards actively oppose. For others, it is because they want to tailor their children's education to their needs or to the family's lifestyle.

Our reason for home-educating our children is that we thought we could accomplish our primary goal for them—that they would love the Lord their God with all their heart, mind, strength, and soul; and love their neighbor as themselves—better than the public or private schools.

SUGGESTED PRIORITIES

Once you have established your primary reason(s) for home-educating your children, you also need to take a look at your priorities. For successful homeschooling, may I suggest you consider the following:

Spiritual health and growth

Your own well-being is a priority, because you can't give what you don't have. Just as we need good food to help us grow, we need to spend time daily with God in prayer and in His Word. His Word renews our minds and restores our perspective to be in line with the Truth. This brings us peace. Not thinking God's way or not living His way results in chaos and stress. It is amazing how much of the world's or the enemy's philosophies, thoughts, and ways creep into *our* philosophy, thoughts, and ways. Reading God's Word regularly *really* makes a difference. While it is fine to read a devotional, it shouldn't be the only source of our spiritual nourishment. Our main source should be the Bible itself.

When Paul writes in 2 Timothy 3:16: "All Scripture is breathed out by God and profitable for teaching, for reproof, for correction, and for training in righteousness," he was referring to the Old Testament, as they didn't have the New Testament yet. Therefore, we should read not only the New Testament, but the Old Testament as well, as it reveals so much about God (His steadfast love, His holiness, His faithfulness, His mercy, His provision, His forgiveness, etc.) and His ways (His care for the poor, the widow and orphan, the foreigner, justice, loving your enemy, etc.).

Chapter 3: Priorities

There are many Bible reading plans available to guide you in reading the whole Bible in a year. It doesn't take that many minutes of your day. In fact, when one reads a chapter from the Old Testament, a chapter from the New Testament, and maybe a Psalm or Proverb as well, one is bound to find a life-giving word, or a timely reminder, and/or something to praise God for.

However, I well know how fuzzy one's brain is in the sleep-deprived years of having a nursing baby and several young ones, one of whom is bound to have a nightmare (and interrupt your sleep) or a health need, such as the stomach flu (and interrupt your sleep), or some other need in the middle of the night (and interrupt your sleep)! In this sleep-deprived condition, one can technically read the Bible, but not have retained one word of it. I am an expert on this! Let me make some suggestions, oh you, my sleep-deprived, fuzzy-brained sisters:

Read the Bible out loud. This really helps focus your attention. While it is ideal to have a quiet time with the Lord before your day begins in earnest (when the children wake up), I have found when I had young ones, that the second I budged in my bed, little children would suddenly show up at my side or on my lap. If this is the case for you, let them crawl into bed or sit on the couch with you as you read the Bible (wherever you are in your reading) out loud with expression. Let them grow up with that image in their minds of Mom reading the Bible first thing in the morning as a living example of what the norm should be.

Another method that has helped me to focus my fuzzy brain is to go through one book of the Bible at a time, summarizing as I read a chapter or a section of a chapter. Having to summarize really demands my attention. In fact, I had read the Bible through many times over the years and wasn't finding it exciting any more, when I began to write down (in my dollar-store journal) a summary of what I read. It is unbelievable what I noticed about very familiar passages/stories that I hadn't previously seen. The Bible came alive to me as I had to engage my mind to do this exercise.

Writing down a verse or a few verses that stand out to you as you read is another way to help you focus. This is less challenging than summarizing, so it engages your faculties somewhat less, but if you are committed to writing down something from the passage you read, it will help you pay attention.

Once you have read, pray about anything that came up in your reading. It is helpful to turn a passage that you are reading into prayer, for example when I read Colossians 3:12–17: *Put on then, as God's chosen ones, holy and beloved, compassion, kindness, humility, meekness, and patience, bearing with one another and, if one has a complaint against another, forgiving each other...* ,I pray, "God, help me to put on, as your chosen one (thank you that I am a chosen one, holy and beloved), compassion, kindness, meekness, and patience. Help me to bear with others and forgive them" (here is where I would get specific if there was someone I needed to bear with or forgive at that time). Pray this out loud — it will help you to focus so that your mind doesn't wander, and you won't get lost in drifting thoughts. How much of my prayer time has been wasted in drifting thoughts!

When reading a Psalm that says, *Blessed be the LORD, my rock,* pray out loud, "Blessed are you my LORD, my rock!" Praying God's Word out loud is helpful, and praying for the needs of the day and the needs of your family (out loud) is helpful as well.

Obstacles and distractions to time spent with God

My youngest is currently thirteen, and I am therefore no longer in that fuzzy-brain season, but there are other distractions. In fact, anything can and will be a distraction. Because of how important it is to nourish our souls and keep growing spiritually, the enemy of our souls will use anything to subtly (and not so subtly) keep us from this most important part of our day.

Many people roll out of bed (or even before they roll out of bed) and look at their smartphones or computers. I used to look at my email as one of the first things I did, but eventually realized that sometimes it meant I answered an email or two and then perhaps spent some time on the Internet, and before I knew it, I had missed my time with God and His Word.

I have since made a commitment to not look at my phone or computer until I have spent time with God. I figure that I need to hear from God before I hear from others. And since I *do* want to hear from others (for example, via email, text, etc.), I make sure that I have spent time with God and His Word first.

I am still tempted to look at my phone when, on the way to the bathroom before reading the Bible I see it lying on the counter where I charge it overnight. Even with my commitment I feel a pull to take it and check for any messages. I usually (although not 100 % of the time) manage to take myself in hand and give myself a firm, "No!"

Is it a sin to look at one's phone or computer before reading the Bible? Absolutely not! But for me, it has proved to be a distraction, so that I won't necessarily have time to spend with God through reading His Word and prayer. Therefore, I have chosen to make this commitment because that is what *I* need to do, to guard my spiritual growth in that area.

You alone know the things that keep you from reading the Bible. May I suggest that you make a commitment to not do any leisure-time or recreational activities until you have spent time with God and His Word? If you spend time with God first, you still will likely get to that book/article/TV show/Facebook/craft/or... but even if you don't, it will not be as great a loss as if you neglected your spiritual life.

Your children's spiritual lives

<u>Reading the Bible</u> with your children near the beginning of the day (this is separate from your own time with God) shows them the importance of it, simply by making it one of the first things you do. It also ensures that you will get that done—as the day goes on there is more opportunity for your plans/schedule to be hijacked (I'll talk about that in the section on scheduling).

<u>Prayer</u> should be age appropriate in length and content. Sometimes I have had everyone do "You are's," which is taking turns, saying to God, "You are____" (Holy, Awesome, Loving, Forgiving, etc.). Other times we do "Thank You's." We also pray for persecuted believers, and many other things, according to needs we know of, as well as our own needs. When the children are old enough, they can be taught "P.R.A.Y." which stands for Praise—Repent—Ask for others—Yourself.

Also, a good habit to get into is to pray about anything that relates to the Scriptures you have read together. This helps make God's Word relevant.

<u>Scripture memorization</u> has wonderful benefits as well. Hiding God's Word in our hearts is more beneficial than jingles from advertising, silly songs, or catchy tunes from a movie.

For many years, I had my children memorize passages of Scripture that I thought would be of benefit to them. We did this all together, but since I was the one holding the Bible, teaching them the new verse and checking what they had already memorized, I was the only one that didn't actually have the passages memorized. When the oldest six were out of the house and I was homeschooling the youngest four, I realized that my youngest son didn't really have the Scripture passages memorized. He was reciting with the others, but was actually a half second behind, counting on the others to move him along. So now I make Scripture memory a part of my one-on-one times with each child, and I have them check me reciting the passage as well, so that I, too, can be memorizing these portions of Scripture. Suggested passages to memorize can be found in Appendix A.

Physical health

Your physical well-being is important. In the season where sleep is scarce, try to develop the habit of napping when the little ones nap. It is more important to use the children's nap time for sleep if that is a need, than to clean the house, or do other things at that time. I used to move heaven and earth to ensure that my toddler and baby napped at the same time, so that I could nap.

When the children outgrow their naps, many mothers have found it beneficial to keep that time designated as a quiet time when the children must stay on their beds and play quietly or read books. This way, you can nap if you need it, or at least have a quiet time as well.

Eat healthy meals, snacks, and drink a sufficient amount of water. Headaches, tiredness, and other unwell feelings can be due to a lack of hydration.

If your children are young, there is a good chance that you are getting sufficient amount of exercise simply by caring for them. It is a good idea to go outside on a daily basis when you can, whether taking the children to the park, playing in the snow, or taking a walk. Fresh air (and sunshine) seems to help everyone.

Marital health

One of the best things that you could do for your children, including the success of their home education, is to have a healthy marriage. Yet so many mothers of several young children have told me: "When my husband comes home from work, I have nothing left to give him."

I understand and can relate to this, because spending all day seeing to the needs of little ones can be so very draining. But while I understand and have been there myself, you don't want to stay there. We can actually do something about it!

Begin by sharing with your husband how drained you feel, and that while you feel depleted, you *want* to have something left for him, because he is important to you. Ask him to pray with you concerning how you can replenish yourself to have something for him, too.

Discuss it together. It is in your husband's best interest to ensure that you are replenished. Perhaps if it is a sleep deprivation issue, he can spend time with the children when he comes home or right after dinner, so you can take a nap. If that isn't your need, maybe you can take a walk by yourself, go grocery shopping by yourself, read a book, do a craft, or whatever it is that replenishes you. It doesn't necessarily have to be every day. It could be a weekly activity. For years, Israeli folk dancing has been a weekly evening activity for me.

This replenishes me! I come home so very refreshed, with renewed energy to give to both my husband and my children.

<u>A weekly date night</u> is a good habit to begin and maintain. It doesn't have to be expensive—many of our dates have been walks. It doesn't have to even be out of the house; if your children are young and you can't afford a babysitter, you can have an in-house date after your children have gone to bed. You can make a special meal with a nice tablecloth and candlelight, or do something else together at home that you both enjoy.

The weekly date night is not the time to talk about the children, family issues, or problems, but to have a pleasant time together, such as you did before you were married when you were putting effort into your relationship. Back then you considered what you would wear (wanting to look attractive), you both put thought into what to do to please the other. It is easy to take each other for granted, but well worth it not to do so.

It *is* important to communicate about and discuss the children, family issues, and problems, but not on your date night—set aside another time for that. To be honest, Alan and I have often begun our date night by talking about current problems, but we are making an effort to set aside another block of time for that. And by the way, no serious discussion should ever happen late in the evening. *Ever!*

<u>Express appreciation to your husband</u>—thank him for all that he does, express appreciation for everything positive about him, and thank God for him as you pray for him daily. Speak favorably about him to your children and to others. This will make a huge positive difference in your relationship.

<u>Do not criticize your spouse</u>, either to others, or dwell on his shortcomings yourself. I know you see his flaws/weaknesses/shortcomings, just as he sees yours—you live with each other! But this is the spouse that God gave you. Focus on his good traits. If there are areas of concern, pray. If you think that there are things you need to address, take the log out of your own eye first (that is, take stock of yourself and be open to seeing how you are doing the same, or similar, things and deal with that) and then speak gently when the time is right, but never late in the day, never when he is stressed, or feeling down already. And don't nag; it is anti-biblical (Proverbs 21:19, 27:15).

<u>For Husbands</u>: While I expect that it is mostly women who are reading this, for those readers who are men, the last two paragraphs apply in reverse, that is: express appreciation to your wife, thank God for her as you pray for her daily. Speak positively about her to

your children and to others. Do not criticize her to others or even in your own heart. When there is an issue to address, do so humbly and gently after taking the log out of your own eye. Communicate with her about how you can help her, as well as how she can help you.

CHAPTER 4: REALISTIC EXPECTATIONS

The sweet, silver-haired lady opened the door and invited me in. Passing over the threshold, I walked into the hushed atmosphere of the home that matched the pristine living room to my right. Not a thing was out of place in this elegant room. We passed on down the hall and I was ushered into a comfortable family room, where peace, cleanliness, and order reigned.

No, this was not a dream. This was what I actually saw and experienced when I went to pray with an elderly lady from our church many years ago. The difference between our two homes couldn't have been greater. But this woman had no children living in her home, in contrast to my half a dozen or so at the time. She was also of different financial means, and had a different personality from mine, meaning that if I ever have no children living at home, and somehow had the means for such a nice house with elegant furniture, my house still wouldn't look like that, because, well…I am me.

One thing that stresses us as homeschooling moms is when we compare ourselves, our children, their education, our families or our homes, to that of our friends (or even strangers or people we read about in magazines or in books like this one) and their children, their home education, their families, and their homes.

DO NOT COMPARE!

God has made you unique. You have gifts, strengths, weaknesses, and a personality that are not someone else's gifts, strengths, weaknesses, and personality. You also have your husband with his gifts, strengths, weaknesses, and personality that are not like someone else's husband's gifts, strengths, etc. And your children are unique in the same way. Your husband's job is different; your relatives are different. I can go on and on, but you get the idea. Each person and each personality is unique and shouldn't be measured against another.

The automatic comparing that women do about most everything needs to go! Make a determined effort, whenever you catch yourself doing it, to stop. Tell yourself: "I am not _____. She is not me. My children are unique, as are hers."

I have a friend named Annie (she has heard me tell this story to every homeschool group that I have spoken to). She has the energy of twenty toddlers and a seemingly infinite amount of gushing enthusiasm. She has done things with her two children such as making telescopes, or ordering painted lady butterfly larvae (caterpillars) that came with special food to study insect metamorphosis (in the cage they made in their living room), observing them complete their development into adult butterflies, while I... haven't.

I have told her that if I hadn't already successfully homeschooled several children before I met her, she would intimidate me. I remember going into her home and her showing me the telescopes that she had constructed with her children. My first response was "I should do that!" And then, "Well, if I only had two children, I could do that." But no. I realized almost instantly that even if I had only two children, I wouldn't do that. I am just not the build-your-own-telescope type, and I am fine with that. I love my children. I love to read to them. I could read to them until I lose my voice. What Annie does is great. I am not Annie. She is not me.

More than once I started to get caught in the comparison trap. Another friend was going to begin homeschooling her children, the oldest of whom was twelve years old. She told me to order for her daughter whatever curriculum I was using for *my* twelve-year-old daughter, so our two eldest were using the same books.

Chapter 4: Realistic Expectations

One day when I was at this friend's house, I saw that she had made tests for her daughter to do at the end of each chapter of her history book. I asked her if I could copy these tests, and I copied the first one. I started having my daughter study for the first test when she had finished the chapter. And then I realized that *my* goal for my daughter at this stage was simply that she would read the material and be familiar with it in a general way. I wasn't trying to make her memorize dates and other facts at that point. But when I saw what my friend was doing, I copied her without stopping to realize (at first) that I was being motivated by an if-she-is-doing-this-I-should-be-doing-this idea, which wasn't a legitimate reason to have my child take a test.

If someone is doing something that fits in with what your goals are for your children, you can learn from them—borrow their helpful idea. But don't imitate someone else without thinking it through, as I started to do.

My do-not-compare advice applies to every other area in life.

Don't compare your husband and his involvement or lack of involvement to other women's husbands. God has given you *this* husband. Appreciate him. Pray for him. Pray that you will be a good wife to him. Pray for him to be a good husband and father. Thank God for him.

Are you aware that it is usual and natural for everyone to show their best face? So, when someone else looks perfect, and their husband looks perfect, and their marriage looks perfect, and their children look perfect, they actually are not. They are not any more perfect than you or me. Don't look at other pastures thinking they are greener. They are not. Every pasture has its green grass and its patches of brown grass. If you are comparing, you are comparing others' green grass with your brown patches, and you are not seeing their brown patches.

Don't compare other people's children to your children, and don't compare your children to one another. Every child is unique (just as you or I) and each one has their strengths, weaknesses, gifting, challenges, personality, etc. Children develop physically, emotionally, socially, spiritually, mentally, and academically at different times. Out of my ten children, some were on the earlier side of learning to read, some were more average, and for some it didn't click until quite late. But once it clicked, that is, once they were ready, they took off and in a very short time caught up to the others.

Some of my children were academically strong—the typical school subjects came easily to them. Others found those academic subjects difficult, but had strengths in areas such as music, dance, or communication. It would be a disservice to my children and serve no good purpose to compare them to each other. Instead, I can appreciate how God has given them their unique strengths.

Life situations are all different. The number of children you have, their spacing, their temperament, the place where you live, your energy level (remember my friend Annie with the energy of twenty toddlers?), your background, your priorities, your husband's job, your husband's temperament and expectations... I could go on and on. No one and no one's situation is identical to that of anyone else, so we *must not compare*.

Homeschooling is a glorious opportunity for you and your spouse to seek God as to what are the priorities for *your* family and *your* children—what they should be learning each year and how. Be open to modifying things as you begin homeschooling each year. As you are going along with your plans, but things aren't working (the curriculum you chose for a certain subject isn't a good fit, or the schedule you figured out needs to be changed, etc.), discuss this with your husband and adjust. You have that freedom. Look at it as a blessing: you are not locked in to anything. It's wonderful!

THE UNINVOLVED HUSBAND

Not everyone reading this book has a husband. In that case, you are more on your own. It would be beneficial to find like-minded homeschoolers and bounce ideas off them. Don't settle for the first homeschooler that you meet. Get to know different ones—there are so many different types of homeschoolers—and build relationships with those who can encourage you in *your* journey.

Others of you have husbands who are okay with your homeschooling, but don't want to be involved. They are fine with your making all the decisions, and would prefer you do so. If that is your situation, then do be extra prayerful. Seek God on your own for your homeschooling questions, and don't burden your husband with things he doesn't want to discuss. Do pray that he will want to be more involved and then when he shows any interest or gives any direction, *welcome his words and ideas.*

THE INVOLVED HUSBAND

Many of us (including myself) think that our ideas are best. I will confess that many years ago, I resented my husband's involvement in my homeschooling decisions. If I wanted to buy a new book or curriculum, I needed to ask my husband and tell him why I thought we should purchase the item, or why we should change a curriculum (we have a standing joke about how many French programs I have bought over the years). I saw that other homeschooling moms just bought what they wanted and made all the decisions and *their* husbands were fine with that. If my husband vetoed something I wanted to do/purchase/change, I resented it. *I* was the one homeschooling, after all. *I* knew best. Eventually I realized that my husband sees things differently. He tends to look at the big picture, and he has wisdom (besides the fact that he has a God-given role as head of the household [Ephesians 5:22-33]).

So, appreciate rather than resent your husband's involvement. And if your husband isn't involved, don't nag, but do encourage him in any interest/involvement he shows.

YOUR HOME

This is another area where it is important to have realistic expectations. You are living in your home all day with little mess-makers. It is not as if you clean the house one evening, briefly tidy up from breakfast, and then everyone heads out to work and school. No, you and your children are at home throughout the day, taking books off shelves, playing with toys, and making other messes. I know (or have heard) that there are people in this world who put each item back in its place after they have finished using it, but try as I might to instill this into my family members' psyche, it hasn't happened yet.

One time my daughter who was a missionary in Haiti and who is extremely bothered by mess was visiting us. To bless her, I tried extra hard to keep the house tidier and cleaner than usual. My children weren't doing school work one morning; they were visiting with their sister. After spending a good part of the morning picking up, cleaning up, and putting away things that various ones had left out, I realized I could keep a perfectly tidy house *if my children were away at school all day.*

This is where *realistic expectations* come in. We need to have standards that fit the situation we are in. If you have three young children including a nursing baby, you should not, nor should anyone else, expect your house to look like a home with three older children. And if you have three older children you shouldn't expect your house to look like a house with no children.

This is also about priorities. Sometimes I choose to spend time with my children instead of cleaning.

Here is where each person/couple/family is different and needs to find out what is realistic for their situation and for their priorities.

CHAPTER 5: GETTING IT ALL DONE (NON-ACADEMIC)

Bleary-eyed Barbara woke to her baby's cry at 5:30 a.m. and stumbled out of bed, scooping the infant out of her bassinette, and slumping with her on the couch. Barbara had already nursed the baby at 11 p.m. and at 2 a.m., and was definitely not ready to be up for the day. After nursing her once again, and changing her diaper, she put her back in the bassinette and crawled back into bed. At 7:30, her three-year-old joined her in bed, and Barbara, after cuddling him for a few minutes, realized that she had better get up and start the day. Her husband had already made coffee, and her five-year-old had set the table with bowls, spoons, and granola. Her husband had put the milk on the table, and poured out orange juice for everyone. Now he kissed them all good-bye and headed out to work. Breakfast eaten, spills wiped up and dishes hastily washed, the baby woke up again and this time was nursed while Barbara read her Bible to herself and the children looked at their children's Bibles and other books. When Barbara was ready, she read from her Bible to the children, and

Chapter 5: Getting it All Done (Non-Academic)

then prayed with them. With her boys needing to get some wiggles out, Barbara made sure they were dressed warmly and then sent them outside to the fenced-in back yard to play, where she could keep an eye on them. She put the baby in the infant seat, put the load of laundry that had been washed the previous evening in the drier and swept the kitchen floor. When the boys came in bright-eyed and red-cheeked, she read to them while jiggling a fussy baby. Then...

Bright-eyed "Morning Mary" woke up at 5:30 am ... on purpose!!! She was a morning person, and on top of that, didn't need as much sleep as the average adult. She made herself some coffee and snuggled up on the couch with a blanket and her Bible, reading, taking notes, praying. She got on the computer and answered email, and when her children eventually woke up she had a hot breakfast ready for them. Her husband was out of town for work, so she led their morning Bible reading (which he did when he was in town) and after praying with her four children (ages 16, 14, 12, and 8) sent them to get ready for the day (which included morning chores). When they were ready, they gathered and Mary read them some history. Then...

Sleepy Samantha's husband woke her up at 6:30 (she never hears the alarm). She was tired, but made herself get out of bed. She took a fruit bowl (from those she had prepared the evening before) out of the fridge, and ate it while emptying the dishwasher and filling her water bottle. She did her morning exercise routine, and now actually feeling awake, read her Bible and prayed. Her three children had woken up meanwhile, and helped themselves to the fruit bowls from the fridge. Samantha encouraged (told) her children to get on with their morning routines of washing, dressing, making their beds, reading their Bibles, etc. And finishing their breakfast, when all were ready, they gathered in the living room where Samantha's husband read the Bible and prayed before going to work in his home office. Samantha gathered her children around the dining room table to do their daily writing. Then...

Routines. We all have them, whether we just fall into them or intentionally plan them out. We wake up and then we follow a similar pattern most days. "Bleary-eyed Barbara" is in that sleep-deprived stage of having an infant who wakes up throughout the night to nurse, and she shouldn't feel that she has to set her alarm and wake up at a certain time. Her children are young, and even the five-year-old only needs twenty minutes of formal academics. But her life still has routine—she gets out of bed after her three-year-old comes in for a cuddle. In my description, it is at 7:30, but that was *that* particular day. Another day it might be a little earlier or later. Her husband has supervised and helped their five-year-old to put breakfast on the table. Barbara lets her boys go out and play while she gets a few quick chores done. And on her day goes.

ROUTINES

The best way to "get it all done"—meaning maintaining your home, keeping up with the laundry, yard work, groceries, meals (and of course, your children's education)—is to have a realistic routine. You already have some sort of routine, and perhaps you can glean from some of the ideas laid out in this chapter, both from my experience and others'.

Some people like to work by a routine that is time-based. Everything has a strict time. When your children are young, there isn't a need for this (although if it works for you, that's fine).

A routine (especially for those with younger children) can be activity based, as in first we do this, then we do that, and then the next thing. That way when one is doing the first thing and enjoying it, one doesn't have to stop just because the clock says so, but one can go on enjoying that activity, book, or whatever.

Maintaining your home

Remember that sweet, elderly lady's home that I described at the beginning of the last chapter? If you have children living in your home, it is not realistic to expect that your home will look like that. And if that is your current goal, then you need to get a different book!

People have different levels of tidiness and cleanliness they can live with, and spouses can differ from one another in this, so it is important to discuss this with your spouse and come to a realistic agreement. If you are in sleep-deprived survival mode, and if your husband's expectations are higher than you think you can manage, then perhaps he can help out more or get you some extra help.

As part of the discipleship of your children, you will want to teach them to help as soon as they are able. "We are a family—everyone helps" should be as normal to them as breathing.

My husband likes to say that in our family we are not co-dependent (with an unhealthy need of each other), nor are we independent (separate individuals who happen to live in the same house), but we are *interdependent* (we all contribute to the family). Children who grow up contributing to the family by doing chores feel useful, which helps them develop a positive sense of worth (sometimes called "self image").

When they are young, they like to be (and should be) around you, and they like to be doing what you are doing, or "helping". While a three-year-old isn't all that helpful, if allowed to "help," she/he will one day (sooner than you imagine) be able to contribute to the cleanliness of your home.

But back to routine. It works well to attach chores to regular happenings, such as mealtimes (or snack times). Plan specific chores for before breakfast or after breakfast, before morning snack, or after morning snack, before lunch, or after lunch, etc.

Kitchen: It works best if dishes can be cleaned, the table and counter wiped, the food put away, right after a meal, or at least as soon after as possible. Let the children help according to their ability, and if they are too young to help, you can give them a dry cloth to wipe a cupboard. Once children are old enough, they can be doing kitchen clean up. A chore chart is helpful if you want to rotate chores. It eliminates squabbling about who does what, as the children have only to consult the chart (which will eventually be memorized).

Helpful Hint: Younger children could have their own special, plastic cup – whether a different colour or different kind. Then, as they have drinks throughout the day, they can reuse the same cup. This not only saves dishes, but prevents the spreading of germs.

Bathroom: As mentioned, the best way to ensure that something gets done is to attach it to something else that *always* gets done, that is, eating! Because cleaning a bathroom takes so little time, you can clean a bathroom immediately after post-breakfast kitchen clean up. Or if you have a morning snack time, you can attach cleaning bathroom(s) to that. Or it can be part of the going-to-bed routine—you can be wiping counters and mirrors while your child is in the bath, or on the potty, or just after he brushes his teeth. This last one is *only for those* whose children who aren't old enough to clean a bathroom. In this scenario, you the mom, end up with little ones in bed *and* a clean bathroom.

If your children are old enough, they should be cleaning the bathroom themselves. There are many cleaning products available that are not dangerous for children (and others) to use.

At times, and with multiple children who were old enough, three of our children were each assigned a bathroom to clean, while another had the job of emptying the trash from all the bathrooms and the other wastebaskets in the house.

One might ask "When is my child old enough?" When our first two daughters were four and three years old, they wanted to be with me while I was cleaning the bathroom, so I gave them a rag and allowed them to "clean" the outside of the tub, to keep them busy (while still being with me). Within a year, they were actually cleaning alongside me. I don't remember at what age they completely took over, but they eventually did.

Bathroom maintenance needn't take long: mirror, sink, and counters cleaned daily only takes a couple of minutes. Toilets can be cleaned once, twice, or three times a week as needed, depending on the traffic. This also doesn't take long. Floors and bathtubs can be cleaned once a week or as needed.

All weekly jobs can be saved for a time set aside each week for cleaning—typically on a weekend when everyone from Dad on down can be involved: dusting, vacuuming, washing floors, bathtubs, etc. And any children that are too young can be playing or "helping" alongside. Helpful Hint: Organizers are your friends: a toilet paper holder/caddy that stands near the toilet, filled with rolls of toilet paper, a mesh bag for bath toys, that hangs on the bathtub faucet, a shower caddy that can hold those things your family uses for baths or showers, and a magazine rack for magazines (or books) if you are a family that has reading material in the bathroom.

Living Room: By living room, I am referring to the area that we do most of our living in. If you have a separate family room where you do all your "living," then this is what I am referring to. We read, play, and do some of our school in this room (and the rest of it on the dining room table). I have heard about a concept called "when-you-take-something-out-put-it-back-when-you-are-done," and I think that it is a wonderful concept, but I have been hard-pressed to make it a reality in the lives of many of my children. Books are taken out and left on couches and tables. Toys or games are taken out and left on tables, or the floor where the children were playing. If this is your reality, then the challenge is to somehow catch the culprits when they have put down the items they have been using to go do something else. But realistically speaking, one usually doesn't witness these events, only the aftermath of many items left lying about.

We either call back the culprit if we know who it is, to put away the item that they left out, or we have a general tidy-up-the-living-room time—before snack, before lunch, etc. If everyone puts a few things away, it doesn't take long. Frequent cleanups are best. This is an uphill battle in our household, but we are gaining ground.

Helpful Hint: A shelf (or however many needed) designated for board games, (whether in the living room or another area), separate bins for separate types of toys (trucks, dolls and accessories, animals, etc.) will make clean-up easier, as well as aid in finding the toy or game that is desired in the future. Note: Toys and such even when theoretically kept in separate bins, eventually will get messy and need special clean-up attention. Because even the best methods are not followed a hundred percent of the time.

Chapter 5: Getting it All Done (Non-Academic)

Bedrooms: The less there is in a bedroom, the less to mess. If possible, keep toys in another more central location (family room? special closet?), where they are played with and where it will be noticed if they don't get put away when the players are done.

Watch for those children who take clothing out of drawers without wearing them, or change frequently throughout the day and leave clean clothing on the floor.

Teach your children from a young age to make their bed as soon as they get up. A made bed goes a long way towards making a room look neat.

Helpful Hint: In our affluent society, we all tend to have too much stuff, even if it is because we have simply been overly blessed with many hand-me-downs. Because every extra item we or our children have is a potential mess, try not to let them fill their rooms, cupboards, and drawers with more than they comfortably need. No one needs ten T-shirts, for example—give some away. Pare down the non-essentials. You can't keep every piece of art and every craft your child has ever made, so take photos of them if you like, and then dispose of them. Keep only the very special ones (in a designated area—maybe a special shelf in their room).

Reality Check regarding house maintenance: Over the years, my husband and I have reminded each other of this verse:

Where there are no oxen, the manger is clean, But abundant crops come by the strength of the ox (Proverbs 14:4).

One might have an immaculate manger if there are no oxen, but as long as there are oxen, the manger will not be immaculate. What farmer, however, would want to do without those hardworking oxen, simply to have a clean manger?

Where there are children (or people?), there *will be* some mess. Without children, we might be able to have an amazingly clean house, but we *want* the children over the childless, immaculate house.

Laundry

Here are three different routines you can choose from to keep up with your laundry:

1. Daily: Put a load in the washing machine every morning just before breakfast. Switch it to the dryer (or hang it up) just before or just after snack time. Fold it and put the clean laundry away after lunch.
2. Daily #2: Put a load in the washing machine in the evening. Switch it to the dryer (or hang it up)

before breakfast the next morning. Fold it and put the clean laundry away after lunch. Note: I was using this method for a while because I lived where electricity cost less during evenings, early mornings, and weekends. So I never did laundry during weekdays.

3. Weekly (usually on a weekend day): Starting in the morning, put a load in the washing machine, and switch it to the dryer when ready. Do as many loads as it takes, either folding the clean laundry as it comes out of the dryer, or all at the end with one massive folding fest!

I have used all three methods and they all have worked in different seasons. The advantage of the weekly method is that I don't have to think about laundry any day, but one. And as it is a weekend day, I am not doing any formal schooling with my children and can do other cleaning, go shopping, etc., putting in loads of laundry throughout the day.

The disadvantage of the weekly method is that if for some reason one's laundry day is hijacked, then one needs to catch up. When that happens, I use the daily method for that week.

Ironing: Happily, we live in an age of permanent press. It seems that 99% of the women I have spoken to over the decades, detest ironing. Many simply do not do it. I have found that if the newly dried laundry isn't dealt with immediately, then even some of the permanent press items need to be ironed. And some of my husband's work clothes need to be ironed, regardless of how diligent I am to remove them from the drier and deal with them immediately. There are two ways to handle this: iron items as needed (that is, when you or your husband need a certain item you or he irons it at that time) or have a certain day every week or two when you do all your ironing.

Helpful Hints: 1) Find a three-sectioned laundry hamper (ours is on a metal stand, with three mesh bags in a row) where you can put dirty laundry in one bag for light, another for colors, and another for dark. Alternately, you can get three hampers, and train your children to know what laundry goes where. This saves sorting when you do laundry, and is invaluable if you are doing a load per day. 2) Make sure you are not washing clean clothes. As mentioned under "Bedrooms," some children have a habit of taking out clothing that they don't wear and it ends up on their floor and then in the laundry. Do your best to break your children of that habit—take a look in their rooms and have them put back all the clothing on the floor that they haven't worn. Also, if they are wearing play clothes that aren't really dirty, they can be worn again rather than be put in the dirty laundry. 3) In our family, each person uses his or her own towel for baths, showers, or washing themselves in the morning, hangs them in their own spot, and then reuses them the next day. There is no using a towel once and throwing it in the dirty laundry. That towel is drying a clean person, and can hang to dry and be reused by that same person. This saves a lot of laundry.

Yard Work: For some, this is the husband's domain, for others, the wife's, and for still others it is shared. I like doing yard work because I enjoy being outdoors especially in decent weather. While many families have a weekend work day in which yard work is done, I have discovered that spending ten to twenty minutes a day weeding, raking, or doing other yard work makes a big overall difference. While it is amazing how quickly weeds grow, it is equally amazing to me how fifteen minutes of weeding can transform a flower bed or a vegetable bed. This year, I made it part of our routine to go outside after lunch and we all worked in the yard or garden for fifteen minutes. Then the children were allowed to play outdoors for a while.

Helpful Hint: If your children are too young to help, get them a plastic rake or plastic tools, and let them "help."

Groceries: Keeping your home stocked with the food your family needs is important and there are so many wonderful ways to do this. It can, of course, be a

Mommy-and-the-kids outing, if that works best for you. Or it can be a Daddy-and-the-kids outing, as you enjoy a time of peace and quiet in your home. It can be a one-on-one time for an individual child to spend with Mom or with Dad, and each child gets a turn week by week. Or perhaps you would enjoy going to the grocery store by yourself, while your husband is with the children. Perhaps it works best for your husband to go by himself. The possibilities are many.

To keep your grocery bill down if you live in a city, look at all the grocery store fliers that come to your door or look online at the grocery stores in your neighborhood and make a list of all the items on sale that you need, by store. There are also apps for smartphones where you can type in an item and it will tell you at what store(s) that item is on sale and for what price.

Then you can either go to the store that has the most items on sale that you need, or if you live where a certain store will price match, you can go to that store and get all the items that the other stores have on sale for those same sale prices.

I will often make a separate trip to a store that has meat at a really good sale, because meat is an expensive item and the savings are big.

Helpful Hint: Keep a shopping list somewhere accessible (perhaps on the fridge) where you write down what you are out of and what you are getting low on. Because I buy some things in large quantities, I always have them on hand...except when I don't. In other words, the items I buy in big quantities last a while, and so I need to note when I am getting low on something and write it down on that list, so that I am not stuck in the middle of my baking and discover that my big flour bins are empty, or that my dozens of eggs are gone, or...!

Meals

Breakfast: To take the stress out of life, simple is usually better. There is nothing wrong with having the same healthy breakfast every day. Perhaps fruit and cold or hot cereal, or fruit and toast with peanut butter. If having the same breakfast is too boring for you and your family, have different fruit, or have one kind of breakfast Monday/Wednesday/Friday and another kind Tuesday/Thursday and spice it up on the weekends. We are all in different stages of life, and there is a stage where to survive without stress, we need to simplify what we can.

Lunch: Leftovers are our friends. With big families, however, there are not often enough leftovers to go around. And if there were, that would be called "supper." Soups, especially in winter, can really hit the spot, but homemade soup tends to take time to make.

When my children were old enough one of them was assigned as her after-supper chore the task of making sandwiches for the family for the next day, along with carrot sticks. The variety was in the sandwiches—one day would be peanut butter, another day egg salad, another day cheese, etc. That way we could be doing our school work right up until lunch time, and then simply pull our lunch out of the fridge.

Supper: The best method I know for avoiding "what-shall-I-make-for-supper?" stress is to plan for the coming week. On Saturday or Sunday, figure out what your suppers will be for the next seven days. For the time that it takes to do that, the payback is worth it, as we all have experienced that "what-am-I-serving-for-supper" anxiety.

Confession: I must confess that most of my supper making in over thirty-six years of marriage has been the fly-by-the-seat-of-my-pants kind, where I decide in the morning (and sometimes later) what we are having that evening for supper. And I have gotten by fine. But I have also done meal planning for the coming week, and it is a wonderful feeling to have my suppers planned ahead. It is a small thing to do that can reduce a bit of stress, unless of course, the thought of planning ahead stresses you, in which case…don't!

When we have company, I like to serve nicer meals (although that isn't necessary). If I have spent more money on such meals (even if it is only because of quantity), I balance it out with inexpensive meals, often meatless, at other times. Some simple and inexpensive recipes, including "company meals" are included in Appendix B.

Helpful Hint: It might be worth your time to plan out a meal rotation, whether a seven-day rotation, or a fourteen-day one. That means (for a seven-day rotation) that every Monday you will have a certain meal (let's say, spaghetti); every Tuesday, fish; every Wednesday, hamburgers; every Thursday, stir-fry; every Friday, chicken, etc. If you are using a fourteen-day rotation, then you would be planning fourteen days of meals that you would continue to rotate. The advantage of this is that once planned, you don't have to think and wonder about what you are serving again.

It is so important to note that whatever I, or any other writer, speaker, or human being encourage you to do, whether regarding the maintenance of your house, keeping up with the laundry, raising and disciplining your children, none of us have it down perfectly or follow our own good plans one hundred percent of the time. We are all on a journey, hopefully growing, learning, doing better—but none of us has attained perfection.

This and other similar books are meant to encourage and help you on the journey. So, when the days don't go as planned, when things don't get done, don't get discouraged, you (and your family) are human just like the rest of us. Tomorrow is a new day.

CHAPTER 6: GETTING IT ALL DONE (ACADEMICS)

"I'm thinking of putting Bethany in school," Ella told me.

"Why is that?" I asked this wonderful and very capable young mother. Bethany was six years old and had two younger sisters, ages three and one.

"I just don't think that I can give her an adequate education with the younger two needing my attention as well" was Ella's reply.

"How has it been going so far?" was my next question.

Ella thought. "Well, Bethany taught herself to read and is reading at a fourth-grade level. Her arithmetic and writing are at a level that is considered normal for her age."

"And you are seeing a problem? I don't quite understand," I told Ella.

"All my homeschooling friends use full curricula with all sorts of science and social studies, plus they do so many extracurricular activities, and I just don't have the energy for all that!" (Note the comparison which was emphasized earlier in this book: "All my homeschooling friends...")

I was able to assure Ella that all she needed for this bright young child of hers was a half-hour a day of formal academics. Besides, she would be bored in school. Ella felt that she could manage a half-hour a day of formal academics and her bright, creative child is not being sent to school to be stifled and bored.

And this is the good news: educating your child at home is not replicating the school institution in your home. All children are different, and we are able to work with them as individuals, teaching them according to their readiness level—holding back if they aren't ready, but letting them forge ahead if they are ready before the "norm"—whatever that is! And when we are teaching one-on-one, or one-on-four (if you are teaching four at a time in one subject), then there isn't wasted time or busy work. So, you and your children can accomplish much more in less time.

Let me illustrate this. Recently I was teaching two of my children about various points of view from which novels can be written (as in first person, "I", or third person, "he"). The curriculum directed the children to pick half a dozen books from our shelves, and see in what person they were written. They each read aloud a line or two from each book, and told me in which person that particular novel was written. This all took about five minutes. In a classroom with twenty-five students, there would not be the opportunity for each child to pick up books and share such things with the class . Or if they all had a turn, it might have taken the whole forty-five minutes to an hour. Or perhaps the teacher would just have to do it all herself—demonstrating examples from various books.

Having done that exercise (which could have taken the whole block of time for that subject in a school setting), we went on to the next concept, and the next.

Do you see how we can accomplish academically what is accomplished in school (and even more) in less time?

I am using the aforementioned curriculum with my fifteen-year-old and my thirteen-year-old at the same time. Once again we see that home education differs from institutional schooling, which is age segregated

One of the things that you can enjoy as you educate your children at home is the learning that takes place together—shared experiences bring the family closer. There are many things that work well this way. For example, after breakfast and some clean-up chores, I suggest beginning each day with a Bible reading (the actual Bible, as opposed to children's Bible stories. Read in an animated way; it is interesting enough. It is not necessary to read a whole chapter or a long portion. Include brief prayers and perhaps Bible memorization.

This is not your personal time with the Lord; it is a family time.

There is no problem with children's Bible Story books as long as they are accurate. Many aren't. But save those for other reading times. Or if you think that your children need the pictures in those books, then you might want to read the story from the children's version, and then read the actual story from the Bible. Children's Bible Story books tend to be limited to the typical Sunday School selection of stories: creation, Adam and Eve, Noah's Ark, etc. Those are amazing true stories to read about, but you will want to read other portions of the Bible as well.

After Bible time, if your children are small, they may need *a time to move*. Action songs that involve the whole body are one fun possibility. Little children will especially enjoy this. "Hokey Pokey" anyone?

Once the children have gotten their wiggles/energy out, you can all settle down to a cozy Mom-read-to-the-children time. Good children's literature, when they are young, such as the *Little House on the Prairie* books, *The Chronicles of Narnia, Heidi, The Railway Children, A Little Princess*, and many others, are so very beneficial. Make sure that you are reading the unabridged versions. Jean Little is an excellent Canadian author that you may not have heard of. You will find some of her books recommended in Appendix C. As your children grow older, you can read something at a higher level, such as Dickens (*A Tale of Two Cities* is my favorite!).

Andrew Pudewa, the founder and director of the Institute for Excellence in Writing, explains that to become good writers, children should have books read to them. He says that it isn't enough to be a good reader, but one must hear the language read aloud. For his explanation, see: http://iew.com/help-support/resources/articles/one-myth-and-two-truths/.

Pudewa suggests that we should be reading books to our children that are above their reading level. Even very young children, who don't appear to be listening, often take in a lot from hearing these books read. This has certainly been true in our household. My eleven-year-old was able to understand *A Tale of Two Cities* when it was read aloud. Do note, he was the youngest child of the group that I was reading that book to. I would not have read it to a group of children if the eleven-year-old was the oldest and a toddler the youngest. For children those ages, I would stick to the first group of books that I mentioned.

Young children can play quietly, if they wish, while you are reading. They will still likely take in quite a bit more than you would expect.

Some might ask, "What if my children can't or won't keep quiet during this time?" I believe that children can be taught to keep relatively quiet for a time. If they have been given some attention and time to be active (see above), then they can be handed some quiet toys to play with, suitable to their age, brought out only for these read-aloud sessions so that they are special. If they insist on making noise, you can explain that you would rather that they stay with you, but if they continue, they will be removed to a playpen in another room. Bring them back after a few minutes, if they are ready to be quiet. This might take several training sessions over some days, but children can learn to be quiet for a while as appropriate (this skill will be very valuable on a great variety of occasions).

After reading aloud, a snack might be in order, perhaps followed by a chore, as that will serve the purpose of getting the children moving, with the benefit of accomplishing some clean up. I permit my son to spend a little time outside playing after snack and doing his chore, as the fresh air and exercise seem to help him focus better.

After that break, you can spend time giving individual instruction as needed, or you can have more group time. I prefer giving individual instruction in the morning and saving other group activities for the afternoon. The reason for this is *Robin's Rule*.

Robin's Rule is not a rule that I made up and enforce, but rather something that I have observed, similar to the law of gravity. My observation is: the first two things we plan in a day get done. The rest...maybe.

Life interruptions seem to happen rather frequently—an accident, someone gets sick, someone outside your immediate family needs you urgently, or simply that one or more of your children are having an attitude or character issue that requires time and attention.

Therefore, whatever I save for later in the day is less likely to get done than the first two things I have planned. And since I believe individual instruction, such as in reading and arithmetic, is very important, I would rather do this before lunch.

As always, this is simply what I recommend; there is no single right way or right schedule for homeschooling. This is one of the benefits of home educating your children: you can tailor-make your plans for your family.

OTHER GROUP EDUCATIONAL PURSUITS

History, geography, science, foreign languages, creative writing, art, and music appreciation are examples of subjects that can be done on a multi-age basis.

Chapter 6: Getting it all Done (Academics)

However, please note that there is no need to do such subjects when your children are young. The natural exploration that takes place when children are playing outdoors—interacting with bugs, sticks and stones, sea shells, trees as the leaves change colour in autumn, seeing a puddle freeze in winter and stomping on it—this is science, and young children don't need anything more at this point in their lives.

Geography is learned naturally when you read stories about people in different places. You can look on a map and show your children where the people whom you are reading about lived.

When you read books about people who lived in a time other than our own, you are reading history. You can look up additional information about that particular time period, in that particular place.

Recently I read a series of books to my children by Rosemary Sutcliffe. These fictional books took place in Britain under Roman occupation and shortly after. The stories were so interesting that it piqued our interest as to what actually happened in British history, so we looked it up. I found a book in the library about the history of Britain and left it lying around for my children to read (a sneaky-mom-trick for mothers with readers: leave books where your children are sure to see them and they will pick them up and read them!).

As the children grow older some of the aforementioned subjects can be pursued in a more formal manner. Perhaps one year you can emphasize science, and another year you can emphasize geography. As they grow older still they can do a lot of this learning on their own. There are many excellent resources to be found.

One group activity that I have enjoyed with my children is what I call Creative Writing. We each (including myself) have a notebook for the purpose. We all sit around the table and write for ten minutes and then read what we wrote. The children enjoy that I actively participate in this writing exercise. While you are all doing this, the ones too young to participate can be given paper and crayons or pencil to scribble with, or if they can speak, they can dictate a story to you. But it is also perfectly all right for them to play on their own.

What do we write about? Sometimes I have chosen three words, or let three children each choose a word, that we all must include in a story. The words are random, having nothing to do with each other, for example: bird, boy, soup. Other times we write about a special day we just had, something about the season we are in, visitors who were over, or about a holiday coming up or one that we just enjoyed. When vacation time is coming up (summer vacation, for example), I have them make lists of the things that they would like to do, so that I can help to make some of those things happen. Sometimes when I am out of fresh ideas for our writing time, I look online. There are many free resources to be found.

INDIVIDUAL INSTRUCTION

Whether after a mid-morning break, or at whatever time you choose, you will want to give your children some individual instruction in areas that are more suited to their particular needs and readiness levels.

It works well to begin this time with your youngest—toddlers and preschoolers. Once you give them some attention, they are more likely to play happily while you give attention to your other children. Read them picture books, sing action songs and rhymes, or do anything else with them that you and they enjoy.

Children at this age are learning so much informally, with no special effort. For example,

"Let's pick three picture books for me to read to you," and then you count, "1, 2, 3."

"Let's put away six pieces of Duplo blocks: 1, 2, 3, 4, 5, 6."

And so on.

When I am toilet training my toddlers, they usually don't want to sit on the toilet as long as I want them to, so I say, "You sit there until I count to twenty. You can count with me: 1, 2, etc." I often will say, "And now we will count to twenty in French: un, deux, trois, etc."

In this way, my toddlers learn to count to twenty painlessly, in both English and French. One doesn't need a formal program to teach them number recognition. There are library books aplenty for this. Or you can casually work this in while coloring, playing with playdough, tracing the numbers in the sand, etc.

While you are giving these little ones some attention, your older ones can be doing individual work as they are able. For example, they can be working on their arithmetic lesson or copy work.

Once the little ones have had their time with you, you can direct your attention to the next oldest, perhaps those who are just learning to read.

Young children (ages 4–8 or 9) need very little in the way of formal academics. It is important to keep in mind that their academic readiness varies quite a bit. Some children might be ready to learn to read at age four or five, others not until six or seven, and still others, even later. Once a child is ready to learn to read, he/she learns to read very quickly. Those children who begin later, learn rapidly and catch up to the ones who began earlier.

You can buy a phonics curriculum to teach a child to read, and that can work well, but you don't *need* one.

Chapter 6: Getting it all Done (Academics)

Some children love this kind of curriculum; for others it's boring. There is also the matter of your budget.

One doesn't need a fancy curriculum to teach a child to read. While fancy curricula can be very nice, they are sometimes too much work for both mother and child. And beware of overkill where you "kill" a child's love for learning. I did this with one of my children early on in my homeschooling career, before I knew better.

A quick teach-your-child-to-read tutorial (To be used at whatever age a child is ready, it could be from four years old at the earliest, up to age seven, on average. There will be exceptions at both ends.)

A first phonics/reading lesson would be to teach four letters to your child—not letter names, but letter *sounds*. You can cut out four square pieces of paper (cutting index cards in half works better as they are more sturdy than paper) and write out one letter per card, teaching the child that "c" says kuh, "a" says "a" (short "a" sound), "t" says "tuh", "s" says "suh", then put three of them together: kuh-a-t—cat and s-a-t—sat. When they understand this concept, then add an mm sound for mm-a-t—mat. That's it. Once it clicks, they can read, and they feel great about that. Add more sounds the next day (b and f), and the following day, and so on. Eventually, you switch the vowel to the short "e" and your child can be reading: s-e-t—set, l-e-t—let, and p-e-t—pet. One can continue on gently, eventually teaching all the short vowel sounds and the consonant sounds. Sight words (those which are not phonetic) such as "a," "the," and "is" should be taught fairly early on so that sentences can be made: "The fat cat sat on the mat." "The pet is wet."

After all the short vowels are learned, teach the concept that each vowel has at least two sounds, that they have learned the short vowel sound, and now they are going to learn the long vowel sound. Now they learn that when you add an "e" to the end of the word, that "e" doesn't make any sound, but causes the other vowel to say its long name: man—mane, hat—hate, hop—hope, fin—fine.

The only resource you need to teach your child to read (as well as do arithmetic and write) for the initial grades, is *The Three R's* by Dr. Ruth Beechick. It was reading one simple article by Dr. Beechick that enabled me to teach my children to read without a curriculum. Hers is not the only book on the market, there are many others that are helpful.

For practice in reading, find readers that use these simple phonics words so that your children can read stories early on in this learning-to-read process. I recommend the "American Language Readers Series" (Volume One is "Fun in the Sun"—Simple Short Vowels), or the "Sing, Spell, Read and Write" readers (if you can obtain only the readers; not the entire package.

While fine, the whole package is not necessary and is quite a lot of work for a young child.)

Regarding arithmetic, by the time your children are four or five years old, they have informally learned to count to ten or twenty. They might even recognize some numbers from books you have read to them or from making them in the sand as mentioned above. Now you can purchase an arithmetic book and they can begin to learn more formally what these numbers look like and to write them (we have enjoyed both A Beka and Math-U-See, but there are many other fine curricula).

Note that while their brains might be ready at this time, often their fine motor control is not. Many of my children, while able to understand arithmetical concepts, were frustrated with trying to write numbers at five years old. They can wait another year.

With little children all the individual, formal education they need (they are learning a lot informally, which we will talk about later) is about ten minutes of phonics and about ten minutes of arithmetic each day. If they want to do more, great! But if not, they are still learning enough with twenty minutes or so of formal academic education.

You can finish off with two minutes of writing, supervising these little ones to ensure that they are learning to form their letters correctly. But do be aware that their fine motor control might not yet be developed enough, in which case, give it another six months to a year. Forming the letters using their fingers in a baking dish of uncooked rice, might be more beneficial for young ones.

When they complete their daily time of formal academics, they can entertain the baby and toddler and you can go on to the next oldest children.

Perhaps these ones are reading, and your time with them can involve having them read to you, after which you can help them learn a new concept from their arithmetic book so that they can complete their next lesson.

As each child is working on his/her arithmetic lesson, you can progress to the next oldest child and look over the work they have been doing, help them in something new, etc.

Older children can do much or most on their own. Your job is to be there to check that all is going smoothly, that they are staying on task, and to help with what they don't understand.

When they are in the later high-school years, and need help in subjects about which you are not knowledgeable (that would be physics for me, or calculus), there are some options. Perhaps it is something that your husband can help with. Also, many of the curriculum providers have a way to contact someone for questions. The Internet has many resources as well. A neighbor has helped with some of our offsprings' higher science and math needs.

When your oldest is four, five, or six

As I have stated many times (and will continue to do so) each child is different. Some are not ready to do any formal learning whatsoever at these ages, and some are so ready that they have taught themselves to read! I have already shared about how young children can be learning things such as numbers and counting in an informal matter. Much learning takes place informally: playing outside, going to the store with Mom or Dad, etc., necessitating very little time in formal academics.

Do you remember Ella, whom I introduced to you at the beginning of this chapter? I had to assure her that half an hour was plenty of time for her to spend with her six-year-old in formal academics. Bethany was reading at a fourth-grade level, and doing writing and arithmetic at her grade level. Besides this, she was learning through playing, making crafts, being in various social settings—church, dance class, playing with her siblings and friends—and most importantly from being around her mother. Ella is exemplary in so many ways, among them in loving, helping and serving others. Simply from being around their mom, her children are learning so many very valuable things that they would *not* learn in a classroom.

Ella had posted a questionnaire on Facebook in which one asks one's child twenty questions and writes down the answers that they give. Four of the answers showed me that no one else but she should teach her children:

- If your mom becomes famous, what will it be for? *Loving her family.*
- What is your mom really good at? *Making people happy.*
- What is your mom not very good at? *Making people not happy.*
- How do you know your mom loves you? *When she reads the Bible with us.*

Do you see what I mean? Note: Ella says that she butts heads with Bethany, and yet those answers were Bethany's immediate responses. Be encouraged. If you regularly conflict with a certain child, don't think that that child doesn't see how wonderful you are, or that you really do love them.

If your child isn't ready to learn formal academics at four, five, or six, don't worry. Keep spending time reading to them, interacting with them, doing informal things, such as counting, in the course of life (e.g. "Let's pick up five blocks to put in the bin"). Now and then, see if they are ready to learn to read by showing them a letter and teaching them its sound. If they get it, teach them another one. If they don't, wait a week or two, or even a month. There should be no pressure on you or on your child. He/she will get it when they are ready. And once they are ready, it will be a lot easier than if they are pushed.

Note: While we (and schools) tend to focus on reading and arithmetic, there are so many other intelligences (music, spatial awareness, interpersonal, etc.) as suggested in this article:

http://www.education.com/reference/article/eight-intelligences/

Some children are very strong in these other areas. The fact that one of my children struggles with algebra does not bother me. Her interpersonal skills are amazing! She is wonderful at being aware of people, welcoming them, building them up, and making them feel special. She is an excellent communicator, strong in music, and has many other strengths.

Let us be aware of and value *all* the strengths of all our children!

CHAPTER 7: LIFE LEARNING

Devorah, my sixteen-year-old homeschooled daughter, sat in the waiting room of the ballet studio. There were still several minutes until her ballet class. A few of her classmates were chatting, some were stretching, and one was doing her homework. Devorah saw the words "Social Studies" on the cover of her classmate's textbook.

"Can I see your book?" Devorah asked the other teenager, and was handed the textbook.

"Social Studies!" she thought to herself. "I've heard of it, but I've always wanted to know what it is!"

She skimmed through the book, and handed it back with a "Thanks!" To herself she thought, "So *that's* what social studies is. I call that 'supper.'"

Devorah told me that story several years after it happened. She was illustrating something I already knew, which is that a great amount of what we know is learned informally in the course of life rather than through formal academics or a textbook.

When Devorah skimmed through the book, she realized that she was familiar with the information in it—mostly from conversations that our family had around the dinner table over the years. We have had informal conversations about politics, about issues that were in the news concerning our country and others, about abortion, and about a great variety of other topics that have come up. This is "Life Learning." Your children *will* learn from life, with or without you. Following are some ways to be intentional about what kind of learning occurs:

LIFESTYLE PRIORITIES

Children will absorb and learn from watching what you do with your time, energy, and money. You can teach one thing, but what they see on a daily basis will influence them more.

What place does the Bible have in your home?

Is it read to the children? Do they see you read it on your own? Do you naturally evaluate things by God's Word? What do you watch for entertainment? What kind of humour do you enjoy? Is how you handle relationships informed by God's Word?

It is important to make the Bible—the *whole* Bible—a priority. The well-known verse: "All Scripture is inspired by God and profitable for teaching, for reproof, for correction, and for training in righteousness" (2 Timothy 3:16) refers to the Old Testament, which was the Bible that Believers had at that time. The whole Bible is filled with truths about God—the Creator, a God of steadfast love and faithfulness, our Provider, the Almighty, in control of all. It also includes practical instructions such as: don't put a stumbling block in front of a blind man (Lev. 19:14), build a fence on a flat roof (Deut. 22:8), return your enemy's wandering animal (Ex. 23:4—a practical outworking of Jesus' "love your enemy" [Matthew 5:44]). It is a very, very relevant and practical book.

Some years, we used the *Bible Study Guide For All Ages* by Dr. Donald and Mary Baker, where one reads a passage and then ask questions about it (meaning the children have to listen). Other years we had a weekly time (for us it was Saturday morning), where we gathered in the living room, and my husband would ask us if we had anything to share from our own individual reading of the Bible during the week. At one point, I gave my children journals and told them to try and jot down at least one verse that was meaningful to them in their daily reading. Some seasons it would only be me and my husband who shared from our daily Bible reading of the previous week, but eventually as the children became older, they would share as well.

Do you have a living relationship with God?

This past year when our local homeschool support group asked me to speak, they asked if my adult son, Daniel, would speak as well. The topic assigned to him was to share what caused him to be proactive about his faith. (Daniel is solid in his faith and has been active in the pro-life movement, ministry to the poor, fighting human trafficking, discipleship, and evangelism).

Daniel shared that his parents taught him not only to know about God, but to know Him. He urged these home-educating parents not just to talk about God to their children, but that they (the parents) should walk with God, seek Him about decisions, trust Him to provide, pray to Him about all sorts of matters, and endeavor to live out His Word.

One important facet of living out His Word, is to admit when you are wrong. Say "I'm sorry" when you fail—and we all do sometimes. When our children see us do wrong, and we are humble enough to admit it and repent, this models a very important trait—humility. "God opposes the proud but gives grace to the humble" (1 Peter 5:5).

When I started Bible College, I was a fairly new believer. I met people who had grown up in Christian homes, but had gone away from the faith for a time. I asked them why they had left the faith, as I was looking ahead to when I would be parenting and wanted to learn from their experience. Almost all of them attributed their departure from the faith to their perception of their parents' hypocrisy—being all spiritual at church, but not at home, and most importantly, not admitting they were wrong and saying, "I'm sorry."

LEARN TO EVALUATE

As you go through your day, interact with things out loud with your children. Ask questions. For example, if you are at a store with your children, and you see another child disobeying his parent, when you leave the store, ask what they thought of that behavior, what they think the child should have done, what the parent should have done, etc.

When you are driving and a car makes a dangerous move, once you calm down, ask why that was dangerous.

Talk about the sermons preached at church (not to be critical, but to be like the Bereans in the Book of Acts (17:10-11). One day on the way home from church, Sarah, our eldest who was a teenager at that time, asked about what a lady had said to the congregation from the front of the church. "That wasn't right, what _____ said, was it?" We agreed that it wasn't Scriptural, and inwardly I rejoiced that she knew the Scriptures well enough to know that what that lady had said wasn't biblical. After all, when people say things from the front it tends to carry weight.

Do you recall what I wrote in Chapter One, when I wondered how my sons received scholarships, despite my feeling as though I had only given them a "bare bones" academic education? We taught our children to read and to think! The examples above are ways in which we interact with our children and teach them to evaluate and to think.

Evaluate movies watched (what are the good and bad values this movie promoted?), commercials or advertisements (how are they trying to make you want to buy their product; are they telling the truth?).

Evaluate the following things, since you, as parents, set the tone by:

Reading. Do they see you reading? What do they see you reading? If reading is a positive thing in your home, your children will likely want to learn to read, or once they do know how to read, they will be more prone to see it as a good thing and do it.

Computer use, cell phone, etc. Do they see you on your devices constantly? They will want to be as well.

Music, What do you listen to? Do you play instruments? Children will imitate.

Other activities. Families have things they value. One family plays a lot of sports or is very active outdoors, another family is more artistic, or musical, or builds things—a fix-it dad will demonstrate by what he does that things can be fixed. Take the children along as much as possible as these various activities and pursuits are learning opportunities.

Because so much is caught rather than taught, it's a good idea to prayerfully take a look at our lives and evaluate them. Seek God for help in dealing with what you think needs to be changed. Husband and wife should be in agreement. For wives, if you think a change, or certain changes need to be made and your husband doesn't agree, pray while making changes where you can in your *own* life. Never nag; it is unbiblical. And don't harp in your heart on negatives regarding your husband. Rather thank God for the positives. Often a husband is more preoccupied with making a living for his family, and other significant matters, while the wife is focusing on the children (which is also *very* significant). Trust God if your husband is not on board with what you see and think, and let it be a matter of personal prayer. Again, always appreciate and respect your husband.

Chapter 7: Life Learning

LOVING OTHERS

Hospitality

God commands it. "Contribute to the needs of saints and seek to show hospitality" (Romans 12:13). Welcoming people into your home doesn't have to be fancy.

Many years ago, one of our children noticed that every morning at a certain time, an older couple used to walk by our house. The children waved at them and it became a morning ritual where someone would actually wait by the window and call, "They're coming!" Our children would all run and gather at the window to wave at them, and they would smile and wave back. One day the couple wasn't there. In fact, they were absent for a couple of weeks. The next time we saw them and waved, they came down our walk and hung something on our doorknob. The children ran down and discovered gifts from the couple's home country, where they had been visiting.

In return, we baked them some treats. The next day when we saw them, we ran outside and gave them these baked goods. They invited us to their home. We went. We invited them over for dinner, but they couldn't come because of English lessons that the wife was taking at that time.

I thought it was a lovely story and told my parents about it. My dad responded by admonishing me not to invite people in to our home because of our dilapidated and uncomfortable couches and furniture. (We were living on not-too-much at that point in our lives; we had recently moved across the country and our furniture was hand-me-downs of hand-me-downs).

I told my dad that people didn't come to our home to sit on lovely furniture, they came for the love that we have to offer. Psalm 68:6 says "God sets the lonely in families" NIV).

The people that need to be welcomed in your home are not coming because they have a need to spend time in a pristine house. They need family; they need love.

Life learning happens when you welcome people from different backgrounds, life experiences, ministries, jobs, points of view, religions. (Debrief and discuss later *if* necessary, with older children ask them questions to encourage them to think.) Children should see love and respect modelled even when we disagree with others. Don't be quick to separate adults from children over a meal; afterwards, if they wish to leave to go play, that is fine. Some of our children used to enjoy staying around and listening to the adults talk, if they didn't happen to have friends their age present.

Look up where a guest is from (afterwards, or while they are there, if appropriate). Perhaps ask the guest about their country (most people like talking about themselves, their country, and their lives).

God's heart for the world

Throughout the Bible we see God's heart for justice and for the poor. Be aware and prayerful about what is going on where you live (abortion, euthanasia, elections, etc.) and elsewhere. Talk about it; pray about it. What does the Bible say? Here is where we can teach our children a biblical worldview. This is where Devorah picked up on social studies. What can you do? You can, and when your children are older, *they can*, write letters to appropriate people, visit your political representatives to talk about an issue, read publications from organizations such as Voice of the Martyrs to find out what is happening with Christians in the world and how we can pray for them. You and your children can make sandwiches for an inner-city mission. Getting together with another family to do this is fun and productive.

LOOK IT UP!

Most of us have access to the Internet at home. If you don't, make use of the library.

Historical fiction is a relatively painless way to learn history. When you read a book to your children, it takes place in a certain time, in a certain location: look it up.

For example, there are many children's books about the Holocaust. My husband and I are Jewish, so this is of special interest to us, but I think it should be of interest to everyone because it is not the only time in history, nor will it be the only time, when one man wanted to take over the world. Lots of good, natural discussion comes from reading such books. In *The Hiding Place*, by Corrie Ten Boom, we read that some Dutch Christians hiding Jewish people from the Nazis thought it was okay to lie to the Nazis: "No, there are no Jewish people here", while others thought they must never lie no matter what. So, we discussed the issue of whether it is ever acceptable to lie. We saw that Rahab in the Bible was rewarded for hiding the Israelite spies and lying about it (Joshua 2).

Movies based on real events. When we watch such a movie, we ask ourselves, "How accurate was it? What really happened?" "Apollo 13," "The King's Speech," "Chariots of Fire," and "42" are all movies based on real people and real events. After we watch the movie, we look up what really happened, or read a book about that event.

I came across a library book that tells the true story of "The King's Speech" and I read it to my children. They had seen the movie with us beforehand, and after we read the book we watched it again, and noted the differences between the two accounts. (Note: there is some serious foul language in this movie, which we fast forward. It is always, *always* good to preview a movie before showing it to your children. This has been a policy with us, and the few times we haven't, we have regretted it.)

By looking things up, you are modelling learning.

*   *   *

A word about the Internet

The internet has a wealth of information, *BUT* it is also a door to much evil. There are about four million porn websites that go looking for you and your kids. Please don't think homeschoolers are immune. We are not. Some basic safety tips: keep your computers in public areas, never behind closed doors. Your children should not have access to the internet without supervision. My husband has set up passwords for various children to allow access to various things. Every computer in your home should have a filter. Be aware of other places where your children might be where there could be unlimited access to the internet, whether the library or a friend's home. For more information on how to protect your family, go to
www.strengthtofight.ca .

An important part of our children's education is to help them learn to sort out fact from fiction. They will come across articles online that appear convincing, but are nonsense at best or dangerous propaganda at worst. Discerning the difference is an important part of learning. Our children should learn how to find original sources of articles, discern heavy bias, and know how to find the original context of quotes.

*   *   *

With anything new that you learn, whether it's how to cook or bake something that you never made before, or how to fix something you've never fixed, or put together something (such as furniture from Ikea) that you've never done, or something for your own pleasure (I am currently learning Hebrew), you are modelling how to learn, and this is caught by your children.

Leave books around. Once children can read, they will often pick up books lying around. They will pick these up even before they can read if they have interesting pictures. Leave books around that are informative and at an easy reading level: children's picture books about famous people, science, or anything.

LIFE SKILLS

Bring children along and involve them as they are able—cooking, cleaning, doing laundry, fixing things around the house, doing yard work, helping Dad/Mom, in whatever ways are possible. Various jobs use critical thinking, math (measuring, counting) or problem solving.

Note: I wrote "involve them as they are able," but it must be as *you* are able as well. Your children don't have to be alongside you at all times. Depending on the season you are in, you might want to do your grocery shopping, cooking, or folding laundry on your own. And that's fine. Your children will have plenty of opportunity to learn without being glued to your side at every moment. Rest assured, as you are home educating them and not sending them off to an institution, they will be with you quite a bit and will learn from you as you and they go through life.

As previously mentioned, arithmetic is a life skill that can be learned at an early age: "I will read you three books: 1, 2, 3;" "Let's pick up seven toys: 1, 2,…7;" counting to 20 in English, then in French or another language, as they sit still on the potty.

Languages are life skills. To be able to communicate in another language opens many doors, whether for ministry, employment, or just blessing someone in passing. If you know a second language, be it French, Spanish, Japanese, or something else, speak to your children in this language from a young age (preferably from birth), and they will learn it with no effort.

While I am fluent in French, it is not my mother tongue, so it was not natural for me to speak it to my babies. However, I can still use French words with them. In fact, I have always used the French word for notebook ("cahier"), so my children thought that that was what a notebook was called and only found out in later years that a "cahier" was the French word for notebook. To spare them this, I could have used the French word and English word interchangeably.

When something bad happened to one of my children, I would say sympathetically, "Le Pauvre!" or "La Pauvre!" ("you poor thing") and so they learned that this was a commiserating thing to say to someone. There was no formal educating or effort involved — this was natural learning.

Some mothers will have a certain time when they will speak only in French, Spanish, or another language, for example, at lunch time.

You can also be intentional by writing a different word or expression on each day of the calendar and using it throughout the day. If you only did that five days a week, that is still approximately 250 new words or expressions per year.

LET THEM BE

Children learn so much just by playing and exploring on their own. When they are little, it is important always to know where they are and what they are doing for their own safety. As they grow, it is good to give them some room and time just to be. While I wrote about how children will learn as they are alongside you and your husband, they do not *always* need to be at your side.

Having a box of old clothes and costumes that they can use to dress up in will stimulate their imagination, as will many other toys such as Lego (the small version of which we didn't have until our last child was old enough for it not to be a choking hazard), Duplo, (the safer, larger version of Lego), Playmobile (which also didn't enter our home until the youngest were old enough for it), and so many other things, such as cardboard boxes or toilet paper tubes

When they are old enough to be responsible and put away their messes, various craft materials can be made available to your children.

Let them go outdoors in a safe environment and they will be creative there as well.

All kinds of learning takes place when you let your children be. Often they will re-enact something you read to them, or something they read or saw. They learn so much from their environment, inside and out.

LET YOUR SCHEDULE GO

Sometimes things will happen in your family or around you (a special event in your city or country) that will be educational, and you can let your schedule go for a day (or however long is appropriate) to take advantage of natural life learning.

For example, the morning after the last Canadian federal election, instead of following our scheduled Bible reading, we read a passage that speaks of God's setting up and taking down leaders. We also read a passage that instructs us to pray for our leaders. Then, we prayed for our Prime Minister whose party would now become the opposition instead of the governing party. We prayed for others in that party who had lost their jobs. We prayed for the new Prime Minister

Following this, I read a transcript of the outgoing Prime Minister's speech and we watched what we could find of it on the Internet. Then we watched the incoming Prime Minister's victory speech.

We spent the rest of the morning writing thank-you letters to our outgoing Prime Minister, for the job he did, and some of us also wrote to another outgoing elected official, as we had a connection to him through one of my sons who had worked for him.

In order to write these letters, we had to look up the correct form that these letters should take, as well as the proper way to address the Prime Minister and the other official.

This was no doubt an educational experience for all, which we would have missed if I had felt that I had to stick to my regular schedule.

LEISURE TIME LEARNING

Each family has things that they do to relax and have fun: games, sports, music, walking or hiking, going to the beach or to the playground. *How* we do these activities forms an important part of our children's education: do we display patience, kindness, good sportsmanship, diligence? Are we training our children to do so? Are we ourselves apologizing when we display impatience? They will need all those traits in their present relationships, as well as for their future ones. They will need these traits when working with others.

LEARNING FROM FRIENDS

One cannot underestimate the power and influence of friends. Your children will learn from their friends, both good and bad. When they are young, you have an enormous amount of control over who these friends are.

One time, we moved to a new city and were attending a church that was filled with homeschoolers. My two oldest daughters wanted to make some friends, so I invited a girl of about their age to our house to play. I overheard quite a lot of attitude—the kind that puts down parents with words and eye-rolling. We didn't cultivate that friendship. As a homeschooling parent, we have a lot of influence over whom our children spend time with, as it often involves making plans, such as inviting a specific person or family over.

We invited another girl over and I heard the same attitude (both these girls were about ten years old). It took some time, but I was eventually able to facilitate the cultivation of friendships with other girls who didn't display that kind of negativity.

At times, I have had to pull back from getting together with certain friends, because I saw one of my offspring adopting a friend's bad attitude and/or behavior. It is not as though my children are perfect angels, but I have enough to do with working on their own wrong attitudes and behavior without having them taking on others'.

As they get older, we can help teach our children to evaluate what makes a good friend and facilitate getting together with them, while hindering the negative friendships. Having no friends is better than having harmful friends.

Chapter 7: Life Learning

We have seen this on several occasions when one or another of our children has gone through a period of time where for a variety of reasons they rarely spent time with friends. We felt sad for one of our sons when he was going through such a season, and yet the outcome was quite positive. He was at an age when the influence of his peers wouldn't have been a positive thing, but would have certainly resulted in increased foolishness! Yet it was not by our design that he did not have many friends. After this season, we noticed his character and maturity level were stronger than they would have been had he had frequent opportunities to be with friends.

I was praying during that time for God to bring him good, godly friends. Eventually He did, and now our son has many good relationships. Of course, in his case, he is blessed with several brothers and sisters, so he did have personal interaction and playmates.

A special word regarding sleepovers. It appears that if parents didn't allow sleepovers, the psychologists/psychiatrists/counsellors would see their caseloads drastically reduced. Sexual abuse is too common when one is sleeping over at a friend's house. The family might be very trustworthy, but besides the fact that 90% of sexual abuse happens with people who are known and trusted, one doesn't know who else might be at that home, who might abuse your child. Yes, sadly, even sheltered homeschooled children have been victims of abuse.

There is no need to panic. Just be wise. Teach your child that no one should ever touch or try to touch or see their private parts (until they are married, of course). If anyone ever does touch them, or attempts to, they need to come and tell you as soon as possible. Assure them that you will never be angry with them. Also, make sure they understand that the words, "Don't tell your mom or dad" or "Don't tell anyone" really mean that they must tell Mom and Dad right away.

A further word on "until they are married" with regard to touching. Too many of our children grow up with the idea that their bodies are bad, sinful, etc. (such as when we try to teach them modesty, or appropriately covering their bodies). We don't want them having these erroneous thoughts. Rather, we want them to think positively of their bodies, while wanting to protect them.

So, be wise: keep your children away from sleepovers.

Summary

You know the Scripture that says, "You shall teach them (God's commands) diligently to your children, and shall talk of them when you sit in your house, and when you walk by the way, and when you lie down and when you rise" (Deuteronomy 6:7). I will tell you my observation. What we are passionate about will be passed on to our children with no effort (just as these verses in Deuteronomy tell us) — this is life learning. I have seen this with a mom who is an amazing seamstress, she loves all things to do with crafts. Her children learn to do these things as she is always doing this for her family, for gifts, or to sell. Another mom is very much into natural remedies — all her children are well-versed in these. A dad is into baseball in a big way — all his children know about baseball, and his sons are baseball enthusiasts as well. Parents who are keenly interested in animals have children who are knowledgeable about animals. There are so many things that you will pass on to your children (both good, and unfortunately not good,) unintentionally.

Life learning will happen and by assessing your priorities and making small or big changes, you can be more proactive about the kind of casual learning that will take place in your children's lives. This learning that I just called "casual" and that I also call "life learning," simply means learning informally as one goes through life, and is *not* to be underestimated. It is valuable learning that is an important part of your children's education. *My encouragement and exhortation* is that you make God and His Word central in your heart and home, so that these will be a priority which is caught as well as taught.

CHAPTER 8: FINANCES

The doorbell rang. I went to answer it. On my doorstep stood a lady I had never seen before.

"Hello," she greeted me. "I just moved into the neighborhood, and I have some clothing to give away. Someone told me that you have a large family. Can I give it all to you?"

"Uh-uh-uh-okay," I managed to say, while thinking, "What in the world?!"

She asked me to come to her car. There were piles of large bags in her trunk (maybe nine?). She helped me bring them into our house. It took a whole day for me to sort through them. The following day was the day my daughter taught ballet classes in our basement studio, and the moms would usually sit in our living room and chat while their children had classes. This time they also looked over the clothing I had been given and took bags home. It was definitely a case of "shopping at home" and it was fun: fun for my children, and fun to be able to give to others, out of the abundance we had received ourselves. God's provision!

God's Word says:

Chapter 8: Finances

Therefore I tell you, do not be anxious about your life, what you will eat or what you will drink, nor about your body, what you will put on. Is not life more than food, and the body more than clothing? Look at the birds of the air: they neither sow nor reap nor gather into barns, and yet your heavenly Father feeds them. Are you not of more value than they? And which of you by being anxious can add a single hour to his span of life? And why are you anxious about clothing? Consider the lilies of the field, how they grow: they neither toil nor spin, yet I tell you, even Solomon in all his glory was not arrayed like one of these. But if God so clothes the grass of the field, which today is alive and tomorrow is thrown into the oven, will he not much more clothe you, O you of little faith? Therefore do not be anxious, saying, 'What shall we eat?' or 'What shall we drink?' or 'What shall we wear?' For the Gentiles seek after all these things, and your heavenly Father knows that you need them all. But seek first the kingdom of God and his righteousness, and all these things will be added to you (Matthew 6:25–33).

God's Word says that God will provide for us as we seek His kingdom. If you are homeschooling because you believe that this is what God would have you do to fulfill his command regarding teaching your children (Deuteronomy 6:6–7), then that is seeking His kingdom, His lordship, and He will provide for you all that you need, and most likely, so much more.

I mentioned in chapter two that while some homeschooling moms work part time, it seems that the majority do not earn a salary. I also gave an illustration of how one mom did some calculations and showed her husband that with the various expenses involved in her working (day care, more/better clothes, transportation to work and back, more fast food/prepared food, etc.), the family would not be significantly better off financially were she to go out and get a paying job.

I would like to address the financial aspect of homeschooling more specifically, looking at various ways to give your children the best, without spending a lot of money.

Much can be done by shopping wisely (e.g. take advantage of sales, avoiding prepared food which tends to cost more, etc.), cooking nutritious, but inexpensive meals, (see Appendix B for some ideas), and purchasing clothing and other necessities in an inexpensive way.

THREE INEXPENSIVE SOURCES OF CLOTHING

1. Thrift stores or consignment stores. The former are less expensive. One can find good quality, gently used items in these stores.

2. Sales. Stores sell clothing for the next season well before that season starts. If you wait until a little while after the season has begun, the clothing will be on sale. You can then buy clothing for the current season at good prices.
3. Hand-me-downs. This might be my favorite. We call it "Shopping at Home." Friends who have older children often hand down their children's outgrown clothing, and we in turn, hand down clothing to others. And of course, we hand down clothing within our own household. (Then there is the random lady coming to my door!!!)

HOMESCHOOLING MATERIALS

There are many lovely, but expensive, educational resources to purchase if you have the inclination and the money.

However, as I have mentioned, many of these are unnecessary. The book I mentioned in Chapter Five by Dr. Ruth Beechick, *The Three R's*, is sufficient to get started with and take you through your children's first few years.

There are also many free resources online.

One can buy used books from homeschoolers.

The local library is another source of books and your library may have inter-branch connections where you can order a book from another library in the city and it will be delivered to your local branch.

You can keep a "Wish List" of books, so that when a relative wants to know what to buy for your child's birthday, you can ask for such and such a book (make sure it will interest your child—no one wants to receive a dry textbook for his birthday).

Some homeschool support groups have lending libraries, and many homeschoolers are willing to lend books to fellow homeschoolers.

Extra-curricular Activities, Various Needs, and Desires

One day my husband, Alan, remarked to me, "Our children live like rich kids." What he meant was that they were taking piano and ballet lessons—something that children on our income at the time didn't normally do.

Our children have been blessed by extra-curricular activities such as the ones he mentioned. In some seasons, we were able to afford to pay for the lessons, but in other seasons, not.

One daughter was able to take flute lessons, in exchange for me providing the flute teacher with a dinner. This was the flute teacher's idea, and gave me the idea of exchanging piano lessons for meals as well. The piano teacher agreed.

Chapter 8: Finances

One year, two of our daughters cleaned a ballet studio in exchange for lessons. Other years, I, as well as several offspring, cleaned the ballet studio in exchange for lessons for another of our daughters.

My children also taught ballet out of our home studio and we used that money for their ballet lessons.

My daughter gave ballet lessons to a friend's daughter in exchange for her dad's giving science lessons to a couple of my sons. Another year, my friend's daughter received the ballet lessons in exchange for the dad teaching my son handyman skills.

At one season in our life, the Lord provided free dental work by a Christian dentist.

We have had seasons where we have been able to afford braces for children who needed them, but we have also had seasons where we couldn't. So God provided through orthodontists who have generously gifted braces to our children. We didn't approach these people. One of our children suffered from crowded teeth. So, I prayed daily for God to either straighten her teeth (he had done that for another of our children) or somehow provide for braces. A kind and generous Christian orthodontist approached us and offered to straighten her teeth for free.

We can't tell God *how* to see to our needs, but we can ask Him to do so. He is our loving, Heavenly Father and ever so creative!

One of my favorite stories is about a young girl named Sara, from a homeschooling family. She wanted to play harp—a very expensive instrument; and harp lessons are even more expensive than piano lessons. Her family's income was not such that they could afford harps and harp lessons, so Sara's mother encouraged her little girl to tell God the longings of her heart. Sure enough, over the years, God provided Sara with harp lessons, as well as with harps loaned to her and harps given to her. She became an accomplished harpist who performs her musical craft.

God provides. He provides all our needs (not always in our way or our timing) and He often provides the desires of our hearts (I believe some of those are desires He has put there).

Another way that God has provided for some, is through part-time jobs that Moms can do from home, whether blogging, selling products, or other online work that can bring in some income.

The key thing is to seek God regarding your finances (as well as seeking Him regarding everything else). Pray with your husband.

God is faithful!

CHAPTER 9: SCHEDULES

The August sun beat down on Samantha's head as she sat at the side of the swimming pool, alternating between watching her son's swimming lesson and trying to figure out a schedule for the coming school year. She had a list of the subjects that she and her husband had decided their children would be studying. In between looking up and watching her son do lengths of front crawl and back crawl, she was contemplating her list and writing down what subjects they could all pursue together, what subject various children could do independently, what subjects various ones would need her for.

"Not unlike a jigsaw puzzle," Samantha murmured to herself as she tried to piece it all together. This year, they would all be doing geography together as well as creative writing, and their usual read-aloud (when Samantha would read great books to her children). Then, while Jeff was doing math independently, she could be helping Ava with French and spelling. While Ava was doing her penmanship and math, she could be helping....

Chapter 9: Schedules

It was a challenge Samantha faced every year, but eventually mastered.

Splash! Samantha's head jerked up.

"Phew!" It wasn't her son. She hadn't missed Jeff's dive.

Routines are something that most people tend to have, whether intentionally, or simply because they fall into them. In chapter five, I suggested some intentional routines to help with life, emphasizing the non-academic things we do.

Scheduling is more intentional, and while we don't necessarily need formal schedules with young children (simple routines will do), as our children get older, we do need to schedule our days to ensure that everything gets covered.

TYPES OF SCHEDULES

There are two main types of schedules: event-oriented and time-oriented.

An event-oriented schedule is easier when you have young children and less work in the way of formal academics. With this sort of schedule, you plan the order in which you are going to do things. For example, after you are awake and have taken care of all your own tasks to prepare for the day (wash, dress, read the Bible, etc.), you might plan that you will all have breakfast, do clean up, read the Bible with your children, read a book to them, go outside, help a child with phonics, do arithmetic, have a snack, and then...This is not based on time, but is still structured.

A time-oriented schedule is more necessary when you have older children and have more formal teaching/learning that needs to take place. In this case, you are planning that at 8:30 such and such will happen, at 9:00, child A works on math, while child B practices piano, as you work with child C, etc.

This detailed planning has you allotting time for all the subjects that your students need to cover, and has you scheduling time to work with one, while others can be working independently.

TIPS FOR SCHEDULING

1. Older children who do most of their work independently can make their own schedule once their parents have discussed with them what they will be studying and what books or learning materials they will be using. If both you and they desire, they can figure this out on their own and present their ideas to you for your feedback and approval. Obviously, they need to know before making their schedule when they are expected to be involved in family learning/activities/chores.

While it is good and right for our children to grow in independence and for us to encourage them in that, they are also a part of the family and that is something that needs to be balanced with that independence. Family is good, family is God-ordained, and we do not want any of our children to lose sight of that in our modern do-your-own-thing world.

2. Pray before you make your schedule, and when done, show it to your husband for feedback. Here is an opportunity to practice humility. Usually when we have made a schedule, we have given thought to it and come up with what we think is best. If our husband points out something that needs changing, that might naturally get our backs up—we're the ones doing it (for the most part) and we know best. Right? Not necessarily. My husband and I have different strengths. He will often point out my lack of margin in my schedule, and I really do need to put more margin in. Or he will ask questions about my schedule that make me think.

3. Once you have tried your schedule for a few weeks, you might see areas that need to be changed. That's okay. As I have said many times before: you have that freedom! Or maybe your schedule works for a few months, but then it needs adjustments because of a change in the baby's nap or due to that part time job opportunity that your teen has. Adjust as needed.

4. Remember "Robin's Rule?": "The first two things you have planned always get done. The rest...maybe."

If you find that certain things just aren't getting done day after day, move these things to first and second place in your schedule for a while. At one point, I had arithmetic and piano practice as the first two things on our schedule (after Bible reading), but I found that we just weren't getting to language arts. So, I switched that and put it first for a while.

Life happens: I have read articles from all sorts of homeschooling moms, including those intimidating ones who seem to have everything under control—scheduling commandos who run their homeschool like an army. Even *they* say that the schedule is a goal (if we aim for nothing, that's what we hit) and is not always (almost never?) perfectly kept. Why? Because life happens—perhaps we are all involved in a learning experience that we don't want to stop (nor should we), or perhaps because of sickness or other needs. Even as I was writing this book, having a self-imposed deadline that I wanted to meet, my elderly mother fell and broke her hip. This involved frequent trips to a city a couple of hours away to help out. This was just days after my son and daughter-in-law had their second baby, their first child still being quite young. So, I have devoted some time to help them out as well. As a result, my schedule has had some adjustments—assigning children tasks they can do on their own while I am not there, and omitting certain things from the schedule on some days. Naturally, my personal projects (this book among them) have had to be put on hold, because more urgent things have come up.

As illustrated, there are plenty of things to "upset" our schedule. My encouragement to you is don't be upset; take it in stride. In our most recent schedule upset, my children are learning how one takes meals to people who have just had babies, they are learning to babysit young children (alongside me, as their "teacher"), and hopefully they are learning to care for loved ones in need. One day they might care for my husband and me.

Every summer I work out my schedule for the coming school year, much like Samantha. I am usually rather proud of the schedules and view them as works of art. But I struggle to stick to them. This could be a side effect of my "laissez-faire," relaxed, laid-back nature. Here are the reasons why I (or you) might struggle with schedules, as well as some responses:

Things change. As mentioned, babies change their nap habits, or I might have a schedule that is based on everyone being awake at a certain time every day, but then one child sleeps in. I have a theory that if someone is sleeping, it is usually because they are tired (or sick), so I don't like to wake a child up. But this does throw off my schedule.

Response: While it is good to plan ahead and make schedules, we need to be realistic, flexible, and adaptable. As I said, if we aim at nothing, we are sure to hit it. It is good to make plans or schedules, but if a baby is cranky and needs attention, we need not beat ourselves up or get discouraged that what we had planned for that time didn't get done. Tomorrow is another day. Taking care of the baby is necessary *and* worthwhile, and something that your other children are learning from as they watch you. This is real life education!

If a child sleeps in and thus our schedule is delayed, decide what thing(s) are not so important for that day and don't do them. Decide what the important things are and aim to get those done. If a child is constantly sleeping in past the time you had wanted to get started, then try giving them an earlier bedtime. Or, you might have to adjust your schedule. *You have that freedom!* Or, perhaps you don't mind waking up that child, in which case your schedule can go on as planned.

I believe in doing something until it's done, rather than stopping just because my schedule says that it is time for the next item on our schedule. I don't feel I need to interrupt what we are doing and go on to that next item.

Response: When you make a schedule, allow enough margin for the planned event or subject to take longer than anticipated some days. Plan a nice amount of buffer time, so that you can complete what you are doing and not feel that you have to interrupt it to go on to the next scheduled subject. On occasion, you can choose to just keep on with what you are doing and not do that next thing that day. Skip it and do it the following day

Being flexible and spontaneous is good to a point. It adds fun to everyone's life. For example, although where we live we have snow for about five months a year, the first time that the fluffy white stuff actually accumulates on the ground is always special. So we drop everything and go out to play in that first snowfall. Or we will go to the beach on a warm, spring day when everyone is in school and we have the beach to ourselves.

Response: A continual diet of spontaneity isn't good for your family in the long run. But go with it now and then to bring joy to your lives—this is certainly one of the wonderful benefits of homeschooling!

CHAPTER 10: ENJOYING IT!

Rita often felt drained as she poured herself out for her family—her newborn, her toddler, and the three children she was homeschooling, while not neglecting her spouse or her home. And yet, when she met people who reacted with disbelief and astonishment upon learning that she not only had five children, but was homeschooling them, Rita would grin and say with all honesty, "I enjoy it! It's the most fulfilling thing I can imagine doing! I'm so blessed!"

Was Rita tired? Yes. But did she enjoy what she was doing? Oh my, yes! (At least, most of the time.)

Before looking at specific ways in which we can enjoy and cultivate our enjoyment of homeschooling, here is a foundation that will give us a helpful perspective:

Romans 12:1 says: "I appeal to you therefore, brothers, by the mercies of God, to present your bodies as a living sacrifice, holy and acceptable to God, which is your spiritual worship."

Presenting our bodies to God as a living sacrifice means that we have given ourselves to God. We are

His. And therefore we are His to direct. Whatever we are doing that is led of Him is our spiritual worship.

Let me illustrate. Many years ago one of my daughters heard an application of this verse as it relates to moms, and shared it with me: If God has made me a mother, then mothering, as I do it in obedience to God, is my worship. It is not the only way I worship God, but it is certainly one of the most, if not *the* most, significant ways. Once I laid hold of this concept, I realized that as I change my baby's diaper, for example, I am doing it in obedience to my calling by God to be a mother. This influenced my attitude even concerning changing my baby's stinky diapers! Sometimes I would sing while doing it, "This is my worship!" My little one would gaze up at me and sing, "Ya-aaa".

Changing diapers became more pleasant as I realized that this was part of my obedience to God, and therefore part of my worship to Him.

Note: If you have a child, he/she was planned by God, whether you intended or wanted to have that child or not. Children don't slip by God as if He were to say, "Oops! I didn't mean for *that* one to be born!" If God has given you children, He planned that, which means you are called to be a mother. Embrace it and mother as unto God! Let it be your worship.

If God has led you to homeschool, then doing so in obedience to God is worship. Realizing that homeschooling, even in the really hard times (especially in the really hard times!), is your worship to God, should help your perspective as you go about your daily responsibilities. You can get out of bed every day, saying, "Here I am, Lord! Another day to worship You in obedience to Your will. Please empower me today to do what you have called me to."

Let us remember that God is good, that He works everything for good. The hard things in our lives are there for many reasons, but one of them is for our good. Our loving heavenly Father is using all sorts of things in our lives (including our children and our homeschooling them) to mold us into conformity to His image, to sanctify us, to make us holy!

Remembering this daily can help us have a positive attitude and enjoy what we are doing. Writing Romans 12:1 out, placing it where we will see it at the beginning of each day, and praying it will help us off to a good start.

I encourage you to pray something such as: "Heavenly Father, I remind myself this morning that I have presented myself as a living sacrifice to You. This is my worship: obedience. Empower me by Your Holy Spirit to do that which you have called me to, today."

Chapter 10: Enjoying It!

MAINTAINING YOUR PRIORITIES

In chapter three, I wrote about the importance of being intentional about your priorities such as your spiritual and physical health, your marriage, and then your children.

In marriage one comes face to face with one's own selfishness in a new way. We now have to consider another person and their desires, their ways of looking at things, etc. It is, to say the least, a growing experience. In a good marriage, both spouses are considering each other, serving each other to the glory of God, as each one endeavors to fulfill their God-given roles and help their spouse fulfill theirs.

Having children is yet another way of bringing one in touch with one's selfishness and sin. If you had asked me before I had children if I was a patient person, I would have said "Oh yes!" Enter colicky baby. I didn't want to be up at 1:30 in the morning with a baby who wouldn't stop crying. I didn't gush with warm, fuzzy feelings of motherhood. On the contrary, I might (read "did") have had a few ungodly feelings on that occasion, as on many others. There were certainly many opportunities to grow in godliness.

As mothers, we serve continually. Taking care of your spiritual and physical health and taking care of your marriage is not selfish. It is what you need to do in order to be able to serve God and your family. Out of your health in these areas, you are able to serve.

My eldest daughter has had a tendency to neglect herself in her service to God and others. When I told her that she needed to take time for herself, she remonstrated. She told me that she was following my example and that she had observed how I had reacted over the years to mothers who talked about needing "me" time.

I quickly explained that the "me time" I was reacting against was not the healthy kind of life (which I write about in chapter three), where one nourishes oneself adequately, gets enough sleep (or tries), has some physical outlet (if you're the mom of small ones, that is sort of built-in), spends time in the Word of God and prayer, and cultivates her marriage relationship. I was reacting to something else entirely, which has selfish roots.

Seek God and discern the difference between a healthy (in all the ways described) lifestyle and a selfish one.

ENJOY THE MOMENTS

Some of us are natural "moment enjoyers" and some of us naturally look ahead, always thinking of future things, possible problems, etc. Here is where the latter need to make some effort to enjoy the moment. There are so many enjoyable moments, and while it is impossible to believe if you haven't been through it, as someone who has graduated eight children as of the writing of this book, let me tell you that those moments do pass and are forever gone. So: enjoy the moments.

What moments? Every possible one, from the way a nursing baby looks up at you while he is nursing, with that "You are my everything" look, to the little hand that grasps yours as you are walking down the hall, or the little chubby arms that hug your neck so tight. The moment when one of your little ones "gets it" and is filled with that sense of achievement, whether it is putting on her own pants, or reading "b-a-t" makes "bat." Cozy times when you are snuggled on the couch reading to your children. The moment when one of your children uses a big word that he read in a book, or when another is able to interact intelligently and politely with an adult. The times you go out somewhere with your teenager and she is glad to be with you and doesn't have the eye-rolling attitude that some teens have with their parents. Life is filled with so many, many of these good moments.

But there are other moments. I have to be honest. There are difficult moments. There are difficult seasons as we seek to train up our children (sinners like ourselves) in the way that they should go. (Prov. 22:6)

How do we enjoy *those* unenjoyable moments, or even whole seasons of difficulty? The answer lies in Hebrew 12:2: "Looking to Jesus, the founder and perfecter of our faith, who for the joy that was set before him endured the cross...." Along with this, heed the exhortation in Galatians 6:9: "And let us not grow weary in doing good, for in due season we will reap, if we do not give up." If you are in a season of difficulty with a child, continue to look to God, do what you know to do, don't give up, and believe God that you will reap.

In every circumstance, we need to cultivate a spirit of thankfulness.

Thankfulness vs. discouragement

While this book is written in order to help and encourage the homeschooling mom, it can be overwhelming if you read it and begin thinking that you have to make changes in a great many areas of your and your family's lives. Instead of feeling encouraged, you might actually feel overwhelmed and thus *dis*couraged!

Pray, and take one, two, or three helpful ideas that you can begin to implement. It is important that your husband be on board, so discuss it with him. Seek God together and prioritize. Remember: God, husband, and children, in that order. This does not reflect the amount of time spent, because you will spend the most time with your children, but your first allegiance is to God and then to your husband. Your children will then do much better.

Remember also that comparison brings discouragement. Don't compare!

We all have areas of strength. Know your strong areas, and be thankful for them—they are gifts from God! Use these areas: capitalize on them. If you are a mom who loves exploring nature, then let that be a big part of educating your children—they will learn so much from that. And you will all enjoy it more than if you try to be someone you aren't. If you are a mom who loves building things, then that could be a great part of your children's education—so many subjects can be covered springing from that ability.

I happen to love reading books to my children, therefore many hours have been spent cuddled up reading to them. Hospitality is a gift God has given me, so my children have benefited from the many varied people we have had in our home for a meal, a night, or a week or two.

You and your children will flourish as you capitalize on your strengths and the way God has made you and gifted you. Your homeschool will be more enjoyable that way than if you try to fit yourself into somebody else's mold.

Exercise Your Thankfulness Muscle. Practice being thankful. Learn to enjoy the people in your life (I'm talking about your children). Do something that you enjoy doing together every day. For me, that would be reading to my children or in the winter, taking them outside skating, or sledding, or building a snowman. For you, it could be something else. Understand that when I or any other writer or speaker say "every day," that's a goal, and when it doesn't happen because life happens—sickness or other interruptions—don't be discouraged, just get back to it when you can.

Sometimes there are seasons when one child or another might be especially whiny, rebellious, or stubborn—"enjoying it" are not the words that come to mind in such a season. When one of our sons was about five, he was naughty all day long. He was constantly being disciplined for his behavior. This went on for weeks. One day as I was putting him to bed, this son said to me, "I am so bad!" My heart broke. "No, sweetheart, you're not bad!" I told him. "We are all sinners and do bad things, but you are not bad!" I tried to help him to understand that he wasn't a horrible, bad person. Later I encouraged my husband to really be on the lookout for any little thing that we could praise him for or opportunities to give him positive feedback. It was difficult. One day I was teaching him to read by the method I referred to in Chapter Six, and he "got it."

That is, he got that "kuh-a-t" spells "cat" and that "b-a-t" spells "bat" and that "s-a-t" spells "sat." His behavior changed immediately. It's as if he had instantly experienced self-worth.

In that season, I had to work hard to exercise my thankfulness muscle, because it was difficult and thankfulness wasn't naturally flowing. What had I to be thankful for? Hmm. That I had a supportive husband. That my difficult son was in a loving home with parents who were trying to be consistent, firm, and loving. That God was my strength. (I wasn't brought up to know God, so how thankful I am that He is now my strength.) That I had hope that God would prevail in my son's life. (He has.)

DISCOURAGEMENT IS REAL

We all get discouraged sometimes, for example, in a season such as the one I have described above. And since discouragement is something that everyone goes through, we don't need to feel awful about ourselves for being discouraged: we are humans. When we are discouraged, however, we aren't looking to God, believing that He can and will help.

Therefore when we feel discouraged, the first thing we should do is talk to God about our situation and ask for His help. Here is an example from some years ago where I was so discouraged, I almost quit! But I learned a lesson that has served me well since then:

One of my daughters, while bright, creative, and often sweet, was also stubborn. Stubborn and rebellious. We clashed quite a bit, since, as her mother as well as her teacher, I was in the position of telling her to do her chores as well as schoolwork. One day, when she was eight years old, I told her what she was to do for arithmetic. "I can't do it!" she whined. "I don't know how!" "Yes you do," I replied calmly. "You have done this kind of thing before." "I can't! I don't know how!," decibels rising. "You can, and you may not have lunch until you finish this," I insisted. It was ten in the morning, and I figured that this assignment should take her a half hour at most. The lunchtime ultimatum seemed most reasonable to me.

For the rest of the morning, she complained, cried, and yelled from her bedroom that she couldn't do it. As I stirred the pot of soup I was cooking for lunch, I was utterly discouraged to hear her carrying on. "I quit!" I thought quite loudly in my head. (I'm not sure what I was quitting, but I certainly felt done.) But then I heard the voice of God. It was not external, but it was more than just a thought in my head. God told me: "Do not grow weary in doing good, for in due season you will reap a harvest if you do not give up." I didn't know that this is a verse in the Bible, until I came across it later: Galatians 6:9.

"Okay," I said, as I stirred the soup. "I'm in."

We ate lunch shortly after that, with my stubborn girl continuing to yell from the bedroom, "I'm staaaaarving!" I felt like a bad mother, not letting her eat until she finished the required arithmetic, but shortly after the rest of us had eaten lunch, she completed the assignment *in five minutes*. And got it all correct!

God was telling me, and His Word tells us, not to give up. Keep sowing, keep doing the good that we know to do, and if we do not give up, we will reap. I took these words to heart, and my husband and I kept raising this daughter and all the rest of our children the best we knew how. Thus, we have reaped a harvest, by the grace of God. It still took several years through much prayer and hard work before something in the heart of this particular daughter changed, but that change did occur and she has become a wonderful, godly person. She regrets the trouble, but is thankful that we did not grow weary in loving and disciplining her. It is this daughter I mentioned earlier who, in her later teen years, encouraged me to regard my mothering as worship.

Side note: when this daughter was a stubborn toddler, someone encouraged me to pray that she would be stubborn for God. I did, and many years later, she is.

Why would I bring up this story of a difficult child, in a chapter on "Enjoying it"? As I have already mentioned, there are difficult times. However, not only can we still enjoy whatever sweet moments there are in a difficult season (and there are those sweet moments), but looking to the future with hope, looking to a season down the road where we will reap in joy for all our sowing in tears, we can maintain a hopeful, positive attitude. Reading the Word of God daily and praying to our loving, Heavenly Father will help us enjoy our calling to homeschool.

To sum up

How we can walk out this amazing calling of homeschooling without anxiety and stress is by thanking God for the gifts he has given us (including our children) and trusting Him to work in our lives and theirs. We need to look at the long term——not growing weary, but having our mind encouraged and renewed by His Word, as well as by our spouses and friends who are on the same journey.

You are working with God to form these human beings that will live forever and worship Him! I would do it all over again in a heartbeat.

Chapter 10: Enjoying It!

What CEO position, what job with a nice big salary with many zeros, could be as wonderful and fulfilling as having a small child put her trusting little hand in yours, or giving your daughter the keys to discovery by teaching her to read, or having a grown-up son thank you for the discipline you gave him for all those years, or having an adult daughter refer to you as her "best friend"? I believe if a CEO could have a taste of these rewarding experiences, she might just leave behind the perks of her job for the privilege of experiencing such a wonderful and fulfilling opportunity.

Be encouraged: you have a worthy and fulfilling calling! Enjoy it!

APPENDIX A: SCRIPTURE TO MEMORIZE WITH YOUR CHILDREN

Some of these passages are only four to seven verses and some are more. It is amazing what a child can memorize, verse by verse. We work on a new verse for several days before we continue. But in the end we have whole passages of Scripture memorized.

Psalm 19	I Corinthians 13
Psalm 23	Galatians 6:7–10
Psalm 46	Philippians 2:1–16
Lamentations 3:20–26	Philippians 4:4–8
Habakkuk 3:17–19	Colossians 3:12–17
John 1:1–17	Hebrews 1–2:1
Romans 12	Lamentations 3:20–26

In addition to the above, for older children:

Psalm 34	Romans 1
Psalm 139	Hebrews 12:1–14
Isaiah 52–53 (or at least 52:13–53:12)	James 1

APPENDIX B: INEXPENSIVE RECIPES

I don't tend to cook by recipe and the amount varies according to family size. So, with the following, you get to fill in the quantities.

MEATLESS RECIPES (WITH POTENTIAL FOR MEAT IF DESIRED)

Note: we have a fresh salad with every meal.

Vegetable and Egg fried rice. Prepare rice as desired (we prefer Basmati rice that we buy on sale in a large quantity, thus it is not expensive.

Scramble as many eggs as will feed your family – 2 per person. Make sure they are in pieces (and not one big clump) Put aside.

Fry some cut up cooking onion. Add to that whatever vegetables you like, sliced carrots, broccoli, peppers, etc.

Add the rice and the eggs, and then soy sauce. Stir.

(One can also add cooked meat, or nuts to this recipe)

Appendix B: Inexpensive Recipes

Lentil soup. Soak 1–2 cups of green or brown lentils in water overnight. Rinse, and soak again (this gets rid of whatever it is that causes gas).

Put lentils in a pot and add two litres (quarts) of water. Boil, then simmer for an hour.

Heat up olive oil (vegetable or canola oil is fine, too), and fry a cooking onion, a couple of green onions or chives, garlic, and dried or fresh parsley.

Add this mixture to the pot that has been simmering for an hour.

When you add this mixture, add noodles—whatever kind you prefer. If you are adding rice noodles, cook them separately and don't put them in with the soup. Put the cooked rice noodles in the bowls and add the soup. If you put rice noodles in with the soup in the pot, they will become too mushy.

When noodles are ready, serve with buns and salad.

Chickpeas and potatoes. Put a few tablespoons of canola or vegetable oil in a pan. Heat it up and stir in some curry powder to taste. Add potatoes that have been diced rather small. Stir. Put lid on pan. Stir occasionally. Peel and grate a large carrot (or a few small ones). When potatoes are tender, add the grated carrot and a can of chickpeas and stir. Add salt and pepper as desired.

Inexpensive Company Dinners

Purchase meat on sale and put it in the freezer. The three following recipes call for skinless, boneless chicken breasts. For the first two recipes, when you take the chicken out of the freezer, let it thaw just enough so that you can cut it into thin slices (not strips!) so that you will have three (or four, if the chicken breasts are thick) that are all the same size and shape as the breast was before you sliced it, only thinner than the original by the amount of times you sliced it. That one breast will feed three or four people! This is what makes it an inexpensive company dinner.

Japanese Chicken. Dip each piece of sliced chicken in egg and then in flour (rice flour if gluten free) and then brown it in a pan in which you have melted butter (or margarine). When the chicken pieces are browned on both sides, place on baking tray. Combine ¾ cup soy sauce, ¾ cup water, 1 ½ cup white vinegar, 1 cup honey and ½ cup sugar (or all honey or all sugar as you wish), and 2 tsp garlic powder (or to taste) in a bowl. Mix well. Pour over chicken and bake at 350° F (176° C) oven for 30 to 45 minutes, basting or else turning chicken pieces over half way

Parmesan Chicken (Regular version). Dip each thinly sliced chicken breast (see explanation for slicing

Appendix B: Inexpensive Recipes

chicken above) into regular flour which you have seasoned with salt and pepper, then into egg, then into seasoned breadcrumbs with parmesan in it. Fry, cooking on both sides. Cover the pan with a lid, to ensure that the chicken is well cooked. Serve with lemon slices that people can squeeze onto the chicken.

Parmesan Chicken (Gluten free version. Season rice flour with garlic powder, onion powder, salt, pepper, paprika, poultry seasoning, and mustard powder. Dip the thinly sliced pieces into this seasoned flour, then egg, then seasoned flour again, and fry on both sides, covering pan to ensure that the chicken cooks nicely. Serve with lemon slices to squeeze onto the chicken.

Sesame noodle Chicken. For this chicken, instead of slicing it as described above, slice thinly width-wise so that you end up with pieces approximately 1½ inch long by ¾ inch wide by ⅛ of an inch thick (or 4 cm x 2 cm x 2 mm). Put these thin chicken pieces into a bowl with corn starch and stir to coat the chicken. Brown the chicken (it really turns white, not brown) in hot oil in a frying pan. Set chicken aside.

Cook noodles (wide rice noodles are nice for this, but any noodles will do) and drain them.

While your noodles are cooking, stir together into a saucepan: Ten cloves minced garlic (I use pre-minced garlic out of a jar, for convenience sake), ¾ cup sugar, ¾ cup vegetable oil, ¾ cup rice vinegar, ¾ cup soy sauce, ¼ cup sesame oil, 4 tsp chili sauce. Bring to a boil, stirring constantly. Place the chicken in the sauce and stir. Then add the noodles and stir. Garnish with sliced green onion and toasted sesame seeds.

Ginger Beef. Use any type of relatively inexpensive steak or roast (not chuck or blade), preferably on sale, that you have frozen. Thaw partially so that you can cut steak into thin slices, roughly the same size as the chicken in the sesame noodle chicken recipe above.

Toss beef in a bowl with corn starch and stir to coat. Brown in hot oil in a frying pan. Set aside. Cut up several carrots into short sticks and chop up 3 green onions. Stir fry the carrot sticks, then add the green onions, about ¼ cup of minced ginger (fresh or from a jar), and 5 cloves of minced garlic (or from a jar). Now combine 3 Tbsp. soy sauce, 4 Tbsp. rice vinegar, 1 Tbsp. sesame oil, ½ cup sugar (or honey) and crushed red pepper flakes to taste. Add this to the vegetable mixture and stir. Bring to a boil, then add the beef. After a few minutes, it is ready to serve on a bed of rice.

APPENDIX C: RECOMMENDED BOOKS TO READ ALOUD

All the books on this list are great for children to read on their own, but they are books that I have especially enjoyed reading to my children. I advise to always screen books before your children read them. When at the library, flip through the picture books they bring you, skimming the pages. We wouldn't give our children food that had poison in it, so why we would we let them ingest what is not good for them in book form? And while most of us allow our children to eat some things that aren't good for them (but not poison) such as candy, chips, or some desserts, we wouldn't let them have a steady diet of those things. Similarly, with books: I believe some "fluff" is all right, but we need to know the difference between fluff and bad content.

I didn't intend to list picture books, but I find that I must mention books by Robert McCloskey such as *Lentil*, *Blueberries for Sal*, *Make Way for Ducklings*, *One Morning in Maine*, and many books written by Shirley Hughes, such as *Alfie Gets in First*, *Alfie Lends a Hand*,

Appendix C: Recommended Books to Read Aloud

Angel Mae, and so many more. There are so many delightful picture books but as mentioned above, many that are not. Do look them over and be discerning as to the values they portray.

This is not a comprehensive list, but here are some novels we have greatly enjoyed.

Twenty and Ten by Claire Huchet Bishop

Charlotte's Web by E.B. White

The *Little House* books by Laura Ingalls Wilder

Books by Walt Morey:
　Gentle Ben
　Year of the Black Pony
　Runaway Stallion

Understood Betsy by Dorothy Canfield Fisher

Books by Geoffrey Trease:
　Cue for Treason
　Word to Caesar
　The Red Towers of Granada

Books by Jean Little:
　From Anna
　Mine for Keeps
　Spring Begins in March
　Look Through My Window
　One to Grow On

Home from Far
Mama's Going to Buy You a Mockingbird
Dancing Through the Snow

The Railway Children by E. Nesbit

Books by Barbara Smucker:
Underground to Canada
Amish Adventure

Books by Elizabeth Enright:
The Saturdays
The Four-Story Mistake
Then There Were Five

Caddie Woodlawn by Carol Ryrie Brink

Books by by Hilda van Stockum:
The Winged Watchman

The "Mitchells" series:
The Mitchells: Five for Victory
Canadian Summer
Friendly Gables

The "Bantry Bay" series:
The Cottage at Bantry Bay
Francie on the Run
Pegeen

The Chronicles Of Narnia by C.S. Lewis (seven books, including *The Lion, the Witch, and the Wardrobe*

Appendix C: Recommended Books to Read Aloud

These books written by Patricia St. John:
Rainbow Garden
The Runaway
The Secret at Pheasant Cottage
The Secret of the Fourth Candle
Star of Light
The Tanglewoods' Secret
Three go Searching
Treasures of the Snow
Where the River Begins

Books by Frances Hodgson Burnett (*note: books by this author have some eastern mysticism in some chapters. Some I choose to skip, and some things I discuss, comparing it to what the Bible teaches*):
A Little Princess
The Secret Garden
Little Lord Fauntleroy

Derwood Inc. by Jeri Massi

Snow Treasure by Marie McSwigan

Books by George Macdonald:
The Princess and the Goblin
The Princess and Curdie

The Silver Sword by Ian Serraillier

The Door in the Wall by Marguerite de Angeli

For older children: all the preceding books, as well as:

These books by Rosemary Sutcliff:
The Eagle of the Ninth
The Silver Branch
The Lantern Bearers
Frontier Wolf
The Shield Ring
The Armourer's House
Brother Dusty-Feet

To Kill a Mockingbird by Harper Lee

The Hiding Place by Corrie Ten Boom

Jane Eyre by Charlotte Bronte

A Tale of Two Cities by Charles Dickens

The Archives of Anthropos by John White:
The Tower of Gebura
The Iron Sceptre
The Sword Bearer
Gaal the Conqueror
Quest for the King
The Dark Lord's Demise

The Seventh World Trilogy by Rachel Starr Thomson:
World's Unseen
Burning Light

Appendix C: Recommended Books to Read Aloud

Coming Day

The Gammage Cup by Carol Kendall

Books by Gene Stratton Porter:
Freckles
A Girl of the Limberlost

ABOUT THE AUTHOR

ROBIN GILMAN is a veteran homeschooling mom of over thirty years. She and her husband, Alan, have been married for over thirty-six years and have ten children, two of them married, and three grandchildren. Robin and Alan have had the privilege of living and ministering (and having children!) in Canada's four largest cities: Toronto, Montreal, Vancouver, and Ottawa, where they currently live. Robin is passionate for the Word of God and her family, which shines through in everything she does. She is a graduate of Ontario Bible College (now Tyndale University College), Toronto, and somehow finds time to write and speak. Visit her website:
www.stressfreehomeschooling.com.

Made in the USA
Columbia, SC
23 April 2018